RIGBY **READS**™
Reading Evaluation and
Diagnostic System

Roger Farr, Ed.D.

Michael D. Beck

Kimberly Munroe, M.Ed.

ISBN 0-7578-9105-5

Harcourt Achieve
Rigby · Saxon · Steck-Vaughn

www.HarcourtAchieve.com
1.800.531.5015

D1361714

Acknowledgments

Editorial Director	Ellen Northcutt
Supervising Editor	Donna Townsend
Editors	Sharon Sargent, Jody Cosson
Associate Director of Design	Joyce Spicer
Designer	Deborah Diver
Associate Director of Production	S. Mychael Ferris-Pacheco
Production Coordinator	Amy Braden
Editorial Services	Tighe Publishing Services
Production Services	Gryphon Graphics

Contents

Get Results! With just a few simple steps *Rigby READS* makes it easy to ensure and document Adequate Yearly Progress!

Step **2**

Step **1**

Diagnose

■ Choose the *Evaluation Test* to determine each student's *Instructional* and *Independent Reading Level.*

OR

■ Choose the *Diagnostic Test* to determine each student's reading level and need for instruction on specific reading skills.

Administer

■ Give the paper-and-pencil test to the entire class.

OR

■ Have students take the online test.

Score and Report

■ Paper-and-pencil tests can be hand-scored or sent to a scoring service. Online tests are computer-scored.

■ Receive computer-generated reports or generate reports for hand-scored tests using the Teacher's Manual.

Match Students to Books

■ The reports identify students' individual skill needs and generate a list of appropriate reading material for differentiated instruction.

■ The *READS* Leveled Book Libraries make having the right materials for each student convenient and easy.

Document Growth

■ Have students take Form B of the test.

■ Document Adequate Yearly Progress.

■ Pinpoint areas for remediation.

Flexible options offer the right solution for you!

Valid and reliable tests provide results you can trust.

Components

Evaluation Test

Find the right *Instructional Reading Level* for all students with the easy-to-administer *Evaluation Test*.

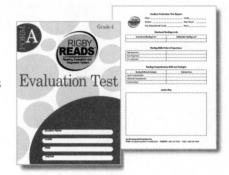

OR

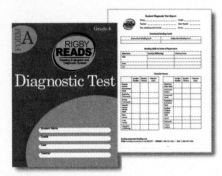

Diagnostic Test

For more detailed information, use the *Diagnostic Test* to identify students' mastery of important reading skills. The *Diagnostic Test* includes the *Evaluation Test*.

Evaluation and Diagnostic Test, Form B

Use the alternate form of the tests to document Adequate Yearly Progress.

Directions for Administering

- Help set the scene for test-taking.
- Provide detailed, easy-to-follow steps for administering the tests.

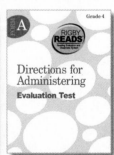

Teacher's Manual

- Background information about each test
- Guidance for scoring the tests and interpreting the results
- Tips for teaching the skills and strategies tested
- Technical information about the tests' validity and reliability

Rigby READS Reports

- Student *Evaluation Test* Report
- Student *Diagnostic Test* Report
- Class *Evaluation Test* Report
- Class *Diagnostic Test* Report
- Student Yearly Progress Report
- Class Yearly Progress Report
- A Letter Home
- Student Test Status*
- Grade Proficiency Report*
- School Proficiency Report*
- District Proficiency Report*

*available with computer-generated reports

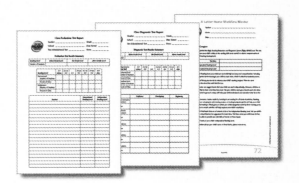

READS Leveled Book Libraries*

- High-interest, enjoyable reading
- Selected to match students' specific reading levels

*sold separately

Rigby READS Online

- All tests and reports
- Call 1-800-531-5015 for more information.

Chapter 1
Introduction to Rigby READS

The *Rigby Reading Evaluation and Diagnostic System (Rigby READS)* provides the information you need to help your students become proficient readers with good comprehension skills. *Rigby READS* provides accurate, dependable data about your students' achievement in the most important areas of the reading curriculum. The data will guide the assignment of your students to the correct reading level and predict success on high-stakes tests.

Here's how *Rigby READS* works:

- Valid and reliable tests accurately measure the reading skills your students need most—including reading comprehension, phonemic awareness and phonics, vocabulary, word part clues, skimming and scanning text for information, and fluency. The tests generate both *Instructional* and *Independent Reading Levels* that accurately show the level of text each student can read with accuracy and comprehension. When students are matched to texts at their appropriate instructional levels, maximum reading progress is achieved.

- Easy-to-follow directions explain the testing process and provide specific information for administering the tests.

- Both the computer program and the scoring service generate reports based on information from the tests. For hand scoring, this manual provides report forms and directions for completing the forms. These reports are useful not only for the teacher, but also for administrators, parents, and caregivers—anyone who has an interest in helping students succeed.

- The Teacher's Manual is planned and written to help you understand the tests and reports and to apply the testing results to guide your instruction. Use this manual before and after testing to learn more about:
  — the structure and special features of *Rigby READS*
  — the content of each test
  — how to interpret and evaluate student performance on each test
  — how to put the assessment results into practice in your reading curriculum
  — technical information about the tests

- The online component of the program provides convenient computer access to tests and reports. Students take the tests online, and the program generates a variety of score reports and planning tools for your use. *Rigby READS* online is available for an additional cost.

The *Rigby READS* Structure

Rigby READS offers you two carefully coordinated test batteries: the *Evaluation Test* and the *Diagnostic Test*.

- The *Evaluation Test* measures growth in reading comprehension, the most important goal of reading. It also provides valid and reliable information for placing students at appropriate *Instructional Reading Levels*.

- The *Diagnostic Test* also measures growth in reading comprehension, and provides additional information about your students' mastery of specific reading skills and objectives.

The *Evaluation* and *Diagnostic Tests* are available for grades 1 through 8, and include a Beginning Reader Test to be used at the end of kindergarten or the beginning of first grade. There are two forms (A and B) for each level, to be used for pre- and posttesting. The Beginning Reader Test has one form.

The *Evaluation* and *Diagnostic Tests* together offer a comprehensive assessment package to meet the varied needs of your students.

The *Evaluation Test*

The *Evaluation Test* contains passages that cover multiple reading levels and a variety of text types. These leveled passages yield a reading comprehension score that represents each student's *Instructional* and *Independent Reading Level*. These reliable and validated scores can be used to match students with leveled readers.

The two forms of the *Evaluation Test* can be used as a pretest and posttest to determine reading growth over time.

The following chart outlines the number of items of the *Evaluation Test*.

Rigby READS Evaluation Test

Reading Comprehension									
	Beginning Reader*	Grade 1	Grade 2	Grade 3	Grade 4	Grade 5	Grade 6	Grade 7	Grade 8
Number of Items	5	44	49	45	48	48	48	48	45

*There is only a Diagnostic Beginning Reader Test.

The *Diagnostic Test*

The *Diagnostic Test* of *Rigby READS* comprises a series of separate tests. Each test represents skill areas within the five elements described in the *Report of the National Reading Panel: Teaching Children to Read (2000)*—phonics, phonemic awareness, fluency, comprehension, and vocabulary. Three more tests in visual discrimination, auditory discrimination, and letter recognition assess students' reading readiness. An additional area, skimming and scanning, has been added to assess students' ability to quickly extract information from functional texts.

Rigby READS Diagnostic Test

	Beginning Reader[1]	Grade 1	Grade 2	Grade 3	Grade 4	Grade 5	Grade 6	Grade 7	Grade 8
Reading Comprehension									
Items	5	44	49	45	48	48	48	48	45
Visual Discrimination									
Items	10	24	12						
Auditory Discrimination									
Items	10	24	20						
Letter Recognition									
Items	10	26	26						
Phonemic Awareness									
Items	40	40	40						
Phonics (Sounds-Letters: Consonants and/or Sounds-Letters: Vowels)									
Items	10	30	57	63	66	66			
Vocabulary in Context									
Items		15	22	22	22	24	24	24	24
Word Part Clues									
Items			21	24	24	18	18		
Skimming and Scanning									
Items							20	20	20
Fluency[2]									

(1) The Beginning Reader Test is only a *Diagnostic Test*.

(2) The Fluency Test is an individually administered test that assesses your student's reading speed, accuracy, and appropriate expression. It is an optional test, available at all levels except Beginning Reader.

Special Features of *Rigby READS*

Leveled Reading Passages Comprised of Various Genres — The Reading Comprehension Test of both the *Evaluation* and *Diagnostic Test* acts as a group-administered silent reading inventory that yields an estimate of your students' *Instructional Reading Level*. The test consists of a range of carefully leveled passages, each followed by items matched to the reading level of the passage. Reading selections include narrative, expository, and functional genres.

Instructional Reading Level— The *Instructional Reading Level,* a criterion-referenced score, pinpoints the optimal reading level at which each student can learn. On page 96 in the Appendix you'll find a Leveling Guide: A List of Reading Level Comparisons that matches your students' *Instructional* or *Independent Reading Levels* to leveled texts. The *Instructional Reading Level:*

- assists you in placing your students in the appropriate reading programs, leveled readers, and instructional groups.

- helps determine the critical skills you will need to emphasize in reading instruction.

- helps determine the most appropriate level of reading materials for each student's independent reading.

Purpose Questions — These carefully constructed organizers precede each reading passage. These questions are designed to help your students:

- focus attention on important elements of the text and activate their background knowledge.

- apply the most effective reading strategies to comprehend each passage.

Link to Achievement Testing — The *Diagnostic Test* complements any achievement-testing program you use. While achievement tests provide a general overview of your students' performance, only the *Evaluation Test* pinpoints each student's optimal reading level for maximum instructional gains while the *Diagnostic Test* provides criterion-referenced, prescriptive information on the performance of each student in terms of specific learning standards for reading. Options for testing include:

- using the *Diagnostic Test* as a pretest for diagnosis and the *Evaluation Test* as a posttest for achievement assessment, or

- using the *Evaluation Test* first for an overview and the *Diagnostic Test* as a prescriptive follow-up for students whose *Evaluation Test* scores indicate a need for additional diagnosis.

Skills in Order of Importance — The degree of importance for each reading skill tested in the *Diagnostic Test* is determined by considering each student's grade placement and *Instructional Reading Level,* and is rated as *Beginning, Developing,* or *Proficient.* A complete table of the importance ratings for all *Instructional Reading Levels* is provided on page 83 in the Appendix. The importance rating classification is based on the degree to which a particular skill is emphasized at various levels of most reading programs.

The importance rating classification is also based on empirical data in which skills tests were administered and scores were matched for thousands of students in a tryout study across the country. The importance classification is therefore based on how students at various *Instructional Reading Levels* actually performed on the skills tests.

Teaching Suggestions — Your students' performance on the *Diagnostic Test* (Beginning, Developing, or Proficient) is based on the total number of correct answers. The Class *Diagnostic Test* Report provides the number and percent of your students in each category. This information will help you set instructional priorities and group your students for instruction.

Untimed Tests — The *Rigby READS* tests can be administered without time limits. However, for classroom planning purposes, the following times are suggested:

Reading Comprehension	35–50 minutes
Visual Discrimination	10 minutes
Auditory Discrimination	10 minutes
Letter Recognition	10 minutes
Phonemic Awareness	15 minutes
Phonics	15–25 minutes
Vocabulary in Context	10–15 minutes
Word Part Clues	10–20 minutes
Skimming and Scanning	20 minutes (This test is timed.)
Fluency	5–10 minutes (This test is timed.)

Attention to Ethnic and Gender Bias — Statistical analyses were made during item tryout to remove any possible item bias. Specific guidelines were used to ensure presentation of both genders in a full range of occupations, roles, and activities.

Parent Information — A Letter Home will acquaint parents with the nature and content of the tests and assist parents in helping their children develop and improve their reading skills.

Chapter 2
About the Tests in *Rigby READS*

Whether your students take the *Evaluation Test* or the *Diagnostic Test*, they will take the Reading Comprehension Test. The *Evaluation Test* consists solely of the Reading Comprehension Test. For grade 5, the *Diagnostic Test* also includes the Phonics, Word Part Clues, and Vocabulary in Context Tests, with an optional Fluency Test. These tests are described in detail below.

The Reading Comprehension Test

Although the Reading Comprehension Test is the first to be discussed, it is the last of the *Diagnostic Tests* to be administered. This is because the Reading Comprehension Test is the longest and, for many students, the most difficult test. It is also the most important test.

The Reading Comprehension Test is the most important of the *Diagnostic Tests* for three reasons:

- Reading comprehension is the best overall assessment of each student's reading achievement.

- The test provides an estimate of a student's *Instructional* and *Independent Reading Levels*. These functional reading levels, particularly the *Instructional Reading Level,* will serve as the basis for interpretation of each student's performance on individually tested objectives.

- The test provides information regarding a student's development on the major comprehension objectives or standards for the grade level.

Comprehension is the goal of reading instruction. Reading is not just pronouncing words; it is relating one's background knowledge to the author's meaning using the printed symbols as cues to that meaning. Although matching sounds with letters, sounding out words, and identifying meanings of words through the use of word parts are important, they are only skills and strategies that help students construct the meaning of printed text.

The *Instructional* and *Independent Reading Levels* are the best indicators of each student's reading achievement. The *Instructional Reading Level* is the single most important piece of information you will need in order to plan reading instruction for your students—individually, in small groups, or as a class. The concept of reading levels is well developed in reading research and pedagogy. Students learn to read by reading, and they need to encounter texts written at appropriate reading levels in order to continue their reading progress and build fluency. Knowing your students' reading levels enables you to select leveled books, independent reading materials, or reading programs that will help your students successfully grow as readers. Reading level information is clearly highlighted on each student's report so that you can create an individualized instructional plan.

The Development of Reading Comprehension

Reading comprehension develops as a reader matures. This development relates to three factors:

- **General Intellectual Development.** As your student increases general knowledge and gains more background experiences, he or she is able to understand more complex ideas.

- **The Ability to Read More Complex Material.** The difficulty of the vocabulary, the length of the sentences, and the complexity of the sentence syntax reflect the reading difficulty of printed text (often referred to as *readability*).

- **The Kinds of Thinking Needed to Understand Ideas in a Selection.** While inferential, critical, and evaluative comprehension should be taught and developed from the first grade on, these skills take on greater importance in the higher grades.

Most reading programs reflect each of the three developmental factors described above. The Reading Comprehension Test is constructed to reflect the common and very logical development of materials found in most leveled reading programs.

How Reading Comprehension Is Assessed

The Reading Comprehension Test is a group-administered test, consisting of a range of carefully leveled passages, each followed by questions gauged to the reading level of the passage. The careful matching of question language and difficulty to reading passage level is one of the unique features of *Rigby READS*. The Grade 5 Reading Comprehension Test consists of nine passages to be read silently with five or six multiple-choice questions per selection. Students can refer to the passages when answering the questions.

The reading passages at a specific grade level are similar in reading difficulty to selections found in basal readers and leveled texts that are designated for the same grade level. This is achieved by controlling vocabulary, sentence and passage length, difficulty of concepts, sentence grammar, and interest level of the topics.

The Grade 5 Reading Comprehension Test contains passages at five reading levels, from grade 3 through grade 7–8. Comprehension Table 1 lists the reading level of each passage and the total number of test items that follow each reading selection.

Comprehension Table 1

Summary of Passage Reading Levels and Number of Items Tested on the Grade 5 *Rigby READS* Test, Forms A and B		
Reading Level	**Passage Number**	**Number of Items**
Grade 3	I	5
Grade 4	II, III	11
Grade 5	IV, V, VI	16
Grade 6	VII, VIII	11
Grade 7–8	IX	5

The difficulty of the test items reflects the difficulty level of the passage. For example, the items accompanying the grade 5 passages can be answered correctly by most fifth-grade students. In addition, these items are easier for sixth-grade students and more difficult for fourth-grade students. These results have been verified by extensive national field testing.

The *Rigby READS* Reading Comprehension passages vary in subject matter to ensure a measure of comprehension on all types of printed material. Comprehension Table 2 shows the classification of text types for the grade 5 comprehension passages. You'll find the following:

- **Expository.** These nonfiction passages replicate textbook reading in a variety of content areas such as social studies and science. Biographies are also included.

- **Fiction.** These passages include narrative works featuring literary elements as well as fables and myths. Descriptive pieces are rich in sensory detail.

- **Functional.** These passages require students to apply reading strategies to common reading tasks, such as following directions, reading letters, and reviewing advertisements.

Comprehension Table 2

Grade 5 Comprehension Passages: Classification of Text Types		
Text Type	**Passage Number, Form A**	**Passage Number, Form B**
Expository	I, II, VI, VII, VIII, IX	IV, VI, VIII, IX
Fiction	III, IV	I, III, V, VII
Functional	V	II

Instructional and *Independent Reading Levels*

Historically, a student's *Instructional* and *Independent Reading Levels* were determined by the use of individually administered Informal Reading

Inventories. These usually consisted of carefully leveled passages that students read either silently or orally. The reading selections were followed by reading comprehension questions developed to assess the student's ability to understand material at the reading level of the passage. The *Rigby READS* Reading Comprehension Test follows the tradition of the Informal Reading Inventory.

The *Instructional Reading Level* is defined as the level at which a student should read for instruction. The material is challenging enough so that some instruction is needed, but not so difficult that the student does not grow as a reader. At this level, the student should be able to comprehend approximately 70% of the material read.

The scores produced by the Reading Comprehension Test are valid estimates of your student's *Instructional Reading Level,* and Comprehension Table 3 provides the score ranges that determine this level. For example, if a student obtains a score of 30, the best estimate of his or her *Instructional Reading Level* would be 5-1.

On Informal Reading Inventories, the material the student reads with ease and efficiency determines the *Independent Reading Level.* At this level the student should be able to comprehend approximately 90% of the material read. Reading material at this level is a good option for the student's choice for independent reading.

Instructional Reading Level (IRL) scores for the grade 5 test range from IRL 2-4 minus to IRL 7 plus. The first number of an *Instructional Reading Level* score indicates a grade level, while the second indicates the range within that grade. For example, 2-1 indicates the lowest range of grade 2. Comprehension Table 3 shows the *Instructional Reading Level* scores for the grade 5 test. See page 96 in the Appendix for information about how the *Rigby READS Instructional Reading Levels* correspond to commonly used leveling systems.

Because the grade 5 test includes passages ranging from grades 3 through 7–8, a student with a very high or very low *Instructional Reading Level* might

Comprehension Table 3

Reading Placement Levels Based on Reading Comprehension Scores for the Grade 5 Test, Forms A and B

Raw Score Range for Reading Level	Instructional Reading Level
0–7	2-4 minus
8–11	3-1
12–14	3-2
15–17	3-3
18–21	4-1
22–25	4-2
26–29	4-3
30–32	5-1
33–35	5-2
36–38	5-3
39–42	6-1
43–45	6-2
46–48	7 plus

need to take another test to accurately gauge his or her *Instructional Reading Level*. For example, the grade 5 test does not contain passages below grade 3, so the *Instructional Reading Level* for the lowest range has been designated IRL 2-4 minus, indicating that the student has an *Instructional Reading Level* of 2-4 or below.

For a student scoring an IRL 2-4 minus, consider administering the grade 4 test to more precisely determine your student's *Instructional* and *Independent Reading Levels*. At the very least, use reading material that corresponds to IRL 2-4 and observe carefully. If the student struggles with the material, adjust his or her reading material and instruction accordingly.

At the other extreme, a student who receives a near perfect score on the Reading Comprehension Test might be reading above the level of the highest reading passage. This student's *Instructional Reading Level* has been designated as 7 plus, indicating that the student has an *Instructional Reading Level* of grade 7 or above.

For a student scoring at the IRL 7 plus level, consider administering the grade 6 test to more precisely determine your student's *Instructional* and *Independent Reading Levels*. At the very least, use reading material that corresponds to grade 7 and observe carefully for signs that the student requires additional challenge.

The Reading Comprehension Test score can provide an excellent guide in selecting and assigning books of an appropriate difficulty level. Some reading programs do not indicate different levels of difficulty within a grade level. For these programs, a score of 30 to 38 would indicate an *Instructional Reading Level* of 5 without reference to easy, average, or difficult. You can probably judge most content-area textbooks to be easy, average, or difficult for your students to read. Use this knowledge in tailoring instruction based on students' IRLs. On page 82 in the Appendix, you'll find *Instructional* and *Independent Reading Levels* corresponding to raw score ranges for the grade 5 test of *Rigby READS*.

Be assured that you can place confidence in an *Instructional Reading Level* assigned to a student whose pattern of correct answers across the graded materials is fairly typical, as described earlier in this section. An atypical pattern would be one in which there are many errors in easier material and surprising success in harder material. Careless errors in the early part of the test may result in an *Instructional Reading Level* that is lower than the student's actual ability.

The test results provide additional information that you can use, together with other data, to formulate an appropriate program for each of your students. Examine and interpret each student's test results and weigh them against your personal knowledge of the student's abilities and day-to-day classroom performance. In the end, all test scores should be tempered by your judgment in forming the basis for the educational plan for each of your students.

Forming Instructional Reading Groups

Rigby READS provides you with the *Instructional Reading Level* necessary for forming reading groups. If you have a large number of *Instructional Reading Levels* in your class, consider grouping students with similar *Instructional Reading Levels,* such as 3-1, 3-2, and 3-3.

Instructional Reading Levels and Reading Skills Priority

In addition to helping you determine the most appropriate level of reading materials, the *Instructional Reading Level* is also the best indicator of the specific skills to teach your students. A student who achieved a given *Instructional Reading Level* has demonstrated the ability to perform certain skills required for reading at that level.

You'll find a complete table of Skills Importance Ratings for each possible *Instructional Reading Level* on page 83 in the Appendix. The skills listed reflect the test names in the *Rigby READS* Tests and the reading skills that are commonly taught in reading programs. If you would like to know specifically how an individual student performs on each of these skills, *Rigby READS* provides such an assessment through the *Diagnostic Test.* Both the *Evaluation* and *Diagnostic Tests* offer a chart that ranks in importance the reading skills that each student needs to develop. The skills are categorized as being of *High, Some,* or *Low Importance* for a given *Instructional Reading Level.* Instructional emphasis on *High Importance* skills best helps the student progress towards achieving the next reading level. Your plan for instruction should be based on a combination of the *Skills Importance Ratings* and the needs of your students.

Purposes for Reading

One of the most important reading strategies your students learn is thinking about their purpose for reading specific texts. Mature readers pick up a book or magazine with a reading purpose in mind. It may be to find a specific piece of information or simply to enjoy a story. In schools, this strategy is taught through prereading activities as students are introduced to a story or a chapter in a content-area textbook.

The *Rigby READS* Reading Comprehension Test includes a single purpose question immediately before each passage. Purpose questions begin on page 92 in the Appendix. Like other prereading activities, purpose questions:

- alert students to the overall topic of the test passages and help them bring to mind background knowledge to better understand the reading selection.

- help students set goals for reading. By considering the purpose questions, students will also be attending to information necessary for answering the test items that follow.

These two functions of purpose questions are supported by schema theory research and recent investigations of the effects of "higher-level" questions in reading comprehension. The purpose questions are categorized according to the type of focus the reader should bring to the passage. The categories are:

- **Comprehending the Overall Passage.** These questions suggest that the reader should obtain a global understanding of the passage and should be able to relate specific details to the overall meaning.

- **Comprehending Specific Details.** These questions suggest that the reader should focus on specific details, memorable facts, and sequencing within the passage.

- **Reasoning.** These questions suggest that the reader should utilize reasoning strategies in order to make comparisons, deduce information, recognize cause-and-effect relationships, sequence stated information, and infer beyond the context of the passage.

- **Reacting Emotionally.** These questions suggest that the reader should react emotionally or respond personally to the material.

Although purpose questions suggest an overall focus for the passages, they do not exclude the reader from gathering other types of information from the passages.

Reading Comprehension Objectives

The Reading Comprehension Test, while developed primarily to provide a valid assessment of *Instructional Reading Levels,* also provides an assessment of reading comprehension objectives grouped into three major categories. For a scope and sequence of objectives tested at all levels of *Rigby READS* and the items assessing each objective, see the Compendium of Objectives Across All Test Levels on pages 88–91 in the Appendix. The following list states the Reading Comprehension objectives that are tested at the grade 5 level. Given a leveled reading selection and questions based on the passage, students are asked to answer questions reflecting these skills or strategies. Information about how a student performs on each of these objectives is provided and can be used as the basis for reteaching.

- Literal Comprehension
    Detail/Sequence
- Inferential Comprehension
    Infer meaning/Cause and effect/Main idea
- Critical Comprehension
    Draw conclusions/Summarize/Analyze story elements/Figurative
        language/Author's purpose/Genres/Facts and opinions

The Phonics Tests

Phonics is the process of matching the sounds of language with letters. The word *at*, for example, has two sounds: /a/ and /t/. The two sounds of *at* are represented by two letters, *a* and *t*. In order to recognize words, readers rely on their ability to match letters with the spoken sounds that are combined to form words.

The Development of Phonics

Students cannot use sound-letter relationships to recognize words (phonics) until they are able to hear separate sounds in words (phonemic awareness). Students will begin using sound-letter relationships to aid in word recognition when they:

- become aware of and can isolate specific sounds; and

- can visually discriminate letter shapes and words in print.

Reading programs generally introduce all or most of the consonant sound-letter relationships in kindergarten or early first grade. The introduction of vowel sound-letter relationships usually follows the introduction of consonant relationships and usually takes place later in first grade. Of course, other word reading skills and strategies are usually taught at the same time so that students learn to apply the sound-letter relationships in the context of reading words, sentences, and short stories.

Sounds-Letters: Consonants

One of the earliest phonic generalizations that children make in learning to read is the matching of consonant sounds with consonant letters in the initial and final positions. For example, what word fits the blank in the following sentence?

Bob hit the _____.

Obviously, there are many possibilities, such as *wall* or *ball*, or even *street*, *roof*, or *brakes*. Notice how the choices are narrowed when an initial consonant letter is provided:

Bob hit the b_____.

When a final consonant is added, the reader is almost certain to know the word:

Bob hit the b_____l.

Mature readers use both phonic generalizations and context clues. They also use the quickest phonic clues available, and these are most often the initial and final consonant clues. Try to read this sentence with only the vowels showing:

_ _ i _ i _ _ o _ ea _ _ _ o _ ea _.

Now try to read this sentence with initial and final consonants.

W _ th _ _ _ _ t y _ _ c _ _ _ d r _ _ d th_s.

The two sentences are:

This is not easy to read.
We thought you could read this.

Students' ability to use consonants to identify words is very important if they are to become efficient and effective readers.

How Sounds-Letters: Consonants Skills Are Assessed

Each item on the Sounds-Letters: Consonants Test assesses students' ability to match the sound they hear at the beginning or at the end of a word with the beginning or ending sound of a printed word. The test measures these objectives:

- Initial Consonants—Students match the beginning sound of the dictated stimulus word to the beginning letter(s) of a printed word.

- Final Consonants—Students match the final sound of the dictated stimulus word to the final letter(s) of a printed word.

- Silent Letters—Students match a silent letter in a printed stimulus word to the same silent letter in another printed word.

For the items testing initial and final consonants, the test asks you to dictate a stimulus word and have the class listen for beginning or ending sound(s). From four printed options, students then select the word that contains a letter or letter combination that matches the selected sound in the dictated word. For example, you might tell your students to listen for beginning sounds and then say the word *star*. Upon hearing the word *star*, students recognize its beginning sounds as /st/ and make the connection between the sound /st/ and the letters *st*. Your students' task, then, is to recognize the first two letters of one of the following printed words:

A stop
B soon
C skate
D tops

The same item format is used for ending sounds.

For the items measuring silent letter recognition, your students will look at the underlined (silent) letter and find the answer choice that has the same silent letter.

knee

A king
B pink
C knit
D keen

Sounds-Letters: Vowels

Using sound-letter correspondences with consonants tends to be more effective in learning to read than does using sound-letter correspondences with vowels for two reasons:

- Students tend to rely on the most apparent clues, and most words begin with consonants or vowel/consonant combinations in which the consonant provides the key to the word's identification.

- Vowel sound-letter relationships in English tend to be less consistent than are consonant sounds. For example, /a/ is pronounced differently in each of these words: sat, far, fate, care and data. Conversely, the same vowel sound can be spelled differently, as the /e/ in he, steal, flee, and receive.

However, the ability to match a vowel sound with the appropriate letter(s) is still an important and effective word recognition skill, particularly when the proper teaching strategies are used. For example, your students have probably learned that in a CVC pattern (consonant, vowel, consonant), the vowel is usually short or unstressed.

How Sounds-Letters: Vowels Skills Are Assessed

The Sounds-Letters: Vowels Test assesses the extent to which students can match vowel sounds with the appropriate letter(s) in the context of real words. First students read a printed stimulus word in which there is an underlined letter or pair of letters that represent a particular vowel sound. Then each student selects the word that includes the same vowel sound from among four answer choices.

To prevent the test from becoming merely a letter-matching task, at least two of the options include the same letter(s) as the underlined portion of the stimulus word. Nearly all the stimulus words and many of the options are at or below the fourth-grade reading level to ensure that the skill being tested is matching vowel sounds to letters.

bead

A bread
B feet
C head
D bed

Four vowel generalizations are assessed on *Rigby READS:*

- Short vowels—Usually, these appear in a CVC pattern and are represented by a single letter. Examples include cap, wet, and bug.

- Long vowels—Usually, these appear in a CVCe pattern and are represented by a single letter. Examples include side, bake, and nose.

- Vowel digraphs—Adjacent vowel letters represent one vowel sound. Examples include meat and should.

- Vowel diphthongs—Adjacent vowel letters represent a combination of two vowel sounds in a single syllable. Examples include round and coin.

The Vocabulary in Context Test

Vocabulary development has a significant effect on students' reading comprehension, and the use of context clues as an aid to vocabulary development is one of the most important reading skills. Although some tests use words in isolation to measure vocabulary development, readers most often encounter unfamiliar words in a sentence or paragraph context. All readers use context clues in reading. Think about the words that might replace the nonsense words in the following sentences:

We had lots of ice cream and phatab at the party.

Tom ran sixty yards around left end and scored a grabnal.

Most people would probably replace the nonsense words with the words *cake* and *touchdown*. While other words are possible, the meaning of each sentence provides a clue to the unknown word. Although context analysis alone will not always enable a reader to identify the unknown word, it does focus the reader's attention on the meaning of the unknown word, greatly narrowing the possibilities from which to choose.

Context analysis can be divided into two categories: the use of semantics (meaning) and the use of syntax (grammar). Although these categories are discussed separately here, semantic and syntactic clues are almost always used concurrently.

Semantic Clues

Knowing the meaning of some of the words in a sentence or selection helps students identify an unknown word. The meaning conveyed by the known words can establish expectations about the meaning of the unknown word. Other sentences that surround a particular sentence containing an unknown word can also provide clues to the meaning of the word. In the sentence, "Roy is standing near the bank," *bank* can be either the bank of a river or a building where money is kept. However, the meaning of the sentence would become clear if it were preceded by a sentence stating that Roy is watching canoes race on a river.

Syntactic Clues

A syntactic clue is obtained from the grammatical relationships among the elements of a sentence. For example, in the sentence, "The _____ is full of water," the word *the* indicates that the missing word is a noun. Because this kind of relationship is obvious to English speakers, it limits the number of possibilities from which to choose. Syntactic analysis is also useful when a single word serves several functions in the same sentence. For example, the newspaper headline *Police Police Police Picnic* uses the same word as a subject, a verb, and an adjective modifying the word *picnic*. The placement of the words helps you understand each word's meaning.

The Development of Vocabulary in Context

The use of context is a natural phenomenon in speech, and your students must learn to use context clues as an aid to word recognition early on in their reading education. Rebus-type sentences are one way to teach beginning readers the use of context to recognize words. In a rebus, a picture embedded in a sentence provides the clue to recognizing the printed words.

Skill in using context clues promotes the development of reading comprehension, and the development of reading comprehension promotes the use of context clues. As your students' reading comprehension increases, so does their reliance on context clues because the vocabulary and sentence structure of the material they read increases in difficulty. By the time your students become mature readers—those who can read fluently at or above a sixth-grade level—they will rely on context clues more than on any other word recognition skill.

How Vocabulary in Context Is Assessed

The Vocabulary in Context Test uses an incomplete sentence format to assess your students' ability to use semantic and syntactic clues. For each test item, there is at least one option, in addition to the correct answer, that fits the syntax but does not fit the sentence semantically. An example of this item type is:

Give _____ a bowl of soup for lunch.

    A more
    B dog
    C eat
    D her

Since difficult words occur in different grammatical positions in a sentence, the Vocabulary in Context Test is divided into clusters by parts of speech. Your students can select the word that best completes a printed sentence in terms of both syntax and meaning. The test includes the following:

- Subjects and predicates

- Adjectives, adverbs, and prepositions

- Direct and indirect objects

The Word Part Clues Test

The use of word part clues is a word recognition skill that involves the division of a word into parts so that it can be understood and read more easily. Word part clues include prefixes, suffixes, inflectional endings, and compound words.

The following sentences illustrate how the use of word part clues can facilitate reading comprehension.

- Jasmine rode her new bike carefully.

  The addition of the suffix –ly to a word means that the word tells how something is done—in this case, carefully.

- The farmer bought the racehorse.

  The words race and horse, when put together, form a new word that describes a special kind of horse—a racehorse.

- Barry was very unhappy when it rained on Saturday.

  The prefix un– added to the beginning of a word usually means no or not—as in unhappy.

The use of word part clues, when combined with phonics, vocabulary, and reading context clues, helps your students comprehend what they are reading.

The Development of Word Part Clues

Word part clues cannot be used as a word recognition skill until students have begun to sound out and read root words. As readers gain skill in using word part clues as aids to word recognition, they become familiar with a greater number of prefixes and suffixes. The difficulty of a prefix or suffix depends on two things:

- the frequency with which it occurs in the reading material

- whether or not it has multiple meanings

At the grade 2 level of Rigby READS, the prefixes and suffixes tested are those that are common in your students' reading and have only one meaning. At the grade 3 and grade 4 levels, some of the prefixes and suffixes tested are less common, although important and useful, and some may have more than one meaning. The Word Part Clues Test at the higher grade levels includes more complex sentences and vocabulary with more difficult word parts than at the lower grade levels. The intent is to assess your students' skill in using word part clues as an aid in reading more difficult material in the higher grades.

How Word Part Clues Are Assessed

The Word Part Clues Test uses an incomplete sentence format for all items, except when assessing compound words. From among four answer choices, your students will select the word that best completes the sentence. This testing procedure is in keeping with the philosophy that word recognition skills must be applied within a given context. An example of this item type is:

Ms. King is our reading _____ .

    A teaching
    B teaches
    C teacher
    D teach

In order to choose the correct answer, your students must be able to identify the root word and the suffix. Because of the importance of the sentence context, the sentences used for the items are at or below the grade level at which the test is normally given.

The Word Part Clues Test also uses sentence context to test knowledge of compound words. In this case, your students choose a word from among four answer choices that, when added to an underlined word in the sentence, forms the compound word that best fits the meaning of the sentence. An example is:

It is Tim's <u>birth</u>_____ now.

    A time
    B boy
    C day
    D fast

In order to respond correctly to this item, your students must know which two words can be put together to make a compound word that makes sense in the context of the sentence. The two root words that make up each compound word are obtained from lower grade level word lists so that they can be easily recognized.

In developing the Word Part Clues Test, a list was compiled of all the prefixes, suffixes, inflectional endings, and compound words found in a number of instructional reading programs. Those affixes and compound words that appear most frequently were selected for this test. The following are assessed on *Rigby READS:*

- Word parts—From among four answer choices, your students select the word containing a word part that best completes a printed stimulus sentence in terms of syntax and meaning.

- Compound words—Your students select from among four options the word that best completes a compound word in a sentence context.

The Fluency Test

Fluency is the ability to read a text accurately and smoothly; at a rate appropriate for the type of text being read; and with the expression and intonation of conversational speech. Fluency is an important reading skill because it provides a bridge between word recognition and comprehension. Research has found that fluency should be taught and assessed if students are to become more effective readers. It is recommended that students receive instruction and practice in fluency beyond the primary grades—especially those students who continue to experience difficulty in reading comprehension beyond grades 3 or 4.

The Development of Fluency

Students who are not fluent readers will benefit from regular practice. Emphasis must be placed on reading for meaning. Rapid reading by itself is not fluent reading. The accuracy, phrasing, and intonation a student shows as he or she reads are important parts of reading fluency. Repeated readings and other guided oral reading procedures improve fluency and overall reading achievement.

How Fluency Is Assessed

The optional Fluency Test within *Rigby READS* is an individually administered oral reading test. The test determines how many words your student can read accurately within a one-minute period. It also provides an opportunity to observe the smoothness, inflection, and expression that characterize your student's oral reading. If a student performs poorly on the Reading Comprehension Test, it is possible that he or she is not reading fluently.

If a student performs well on the Reading Comprehension Test, it is likely that he or she is already a fluent reader. However, since fluency is so closely linked to comprehension, it is not unreasonable to test any student whom you feel is having difficulty with fluency.

General Directions for Administering the Fluency Test

Specific directions for administering the Fluency Test are in the Appendix. The following general directions are provided as an overview of the test and how it should be administered.

Have the student practice reading the test a few times before you administer it. The Fluency Test consists of a passage that your student will read aloud while you record the following:

■ the total number of words the student read in a one-minute period;

- the number of errors the student made during the same one-minute period;

- the number of words correct per minute (total number of words read minus the number of errors, which comprises the student's score on the test);

- observations about the student's smoothness, inflection, and expression during reading;

- the student's rank on the reading fluency scale.

The Fluency Test and Directions are provided as blackline masters on pages 66–68 in the Appendix. The Fluency Test is to be administered one-on-one. Provide each student with a copy of the passage that he or she is to read. Use a separate copy to follow along and record observations and scoring information. Work with test takers at the back of your classroom or another place that is quiet and removed from general activity. Be sure to put the test taker at ease. You will want to plan an activity for the rest of the class during periods in which you administer the Fluency Test to some students individually.

To provide a standardized format for the test, an on-grade-level test is provided in this manual. However, for students who are reading well below grade level, you might want to consider administering a lower level of the Fluency Test. Additionally, you may want to administer the Fluency Test again near the end of the school year in order to measure students' progress.

Chapter 3
Scoring and Report Forms

Scanning and Scoring the Tests

There are three ways to score the test:

- Computer Scoring
- Hand Scoring
- Scoring Service

Computer Scoring

When a student takes the *Rigby READS* Test using a computer, the student sends the test to be scored by clicking "OK" in the dialog box that asks "Are you sure you want to send your test to your teacher?"

Of all of the scoring methods, computer scoring provides the most options for generating reports. You, the teacher, will see the scores when you select the Reports tab on the main screen. The reports that can be generated from computer-administered tests include the following:

- Student *Evaluation Test* Report
- Student *Diagnostic Test* Report
- Class *Evaluation Test* Report
- Class *Diagnostic Test* Report
- Student Yearly Progress Report
- Class Yearly Progress Report
- A Letter Home
- Student Test Status
- Grade Proficiency Report
- School Proficiency Report
- District Proficiency Report

All reports are described on pages 31–43. For more information about *Rigby READS* Online, call 1-800-531-5015.

Hand Scoring

If students take the paper-and-pencil form of the *Rigby READS* test, you have two options for scoring:

■ You can score the tests by hand, or

■ you can send the tests to a scoring service.

This section describes how to score the test by hand and how to fill out the resulting report. The report includes only raw scores for the student.

Before Hand Scoring

1. Make sure that you have the correct set of answer keys for the test you are going to score. The answer keys for the *Evaluation Tests* are on pages 69 and 71 in the Appendix and the answer keys for all of the tests in the *Diagnostic Tests* are on pages 70 and 72. You can make an answer key master by completing an Answer Document with the correct answers and then making a photocopy on heavy paper or acetate. Punch a hole through each correctly marked answer on your answer key master.

2. Before using the answer key master, check each booklet or answer sheet for items that have more than one answer space marked. Then draw a red line through all of the answer spaces for items that have more than one answer space marked. If it is obvious that the student had intended to change the answer (for example, if one answer is incompletely erased), choose the final answer as the one to be scored.

3. You should only score tests that have been attempted. A test is considered to be attempted if the student has marked an answer to at least three of the first six items, regardless of the correctness of the responses.

If a test has been attempted, but there are no correct responses, a raw score of zero should be recorded.

Scoring the Tests

To score the test, count the number of marked answers that appear through the holes in the perforated answer key master.

1. Open all answer documents and score them with the answer key master.

2. Use a brightly colored pen to mark each wrong response through the hole in the key. This makes it easier to see which questions were missed and which were answered correctly.

3. To make sure that the scores are accurate, have a second person rescore a sample of the set of tests. If there are scoring errors, rescore the entire set of tests.

Creating Reports

1. When each answer sheet has been checked, write the number of correct answers for each test at the edge of the page. This is the raw score.

2. After you have the raw score, you can use the tables on pages 82–87 in the Appendix to create the Student *Evaluation Test* Report and Student *Diagnostic Test* Report. The report forms are on pages 73 and 75. Here are some examples:

   - **To fill in the Functional Reading Levels Chart** — If a student scores 36 on the Reading Comprehension Test/*Evaluation Test*, look at the *Instructional* and *Independent Reading Level* Cut Scores for the grade 5 test on page 82. Find the column for Cut Score for *Instructional Reading Level*. You'll see that a raw score of 36 transfers to an *Instructional Reading Level* of 5-3 and an *Independent Reading Level* of 4-3. You can now fill in the Functional Reading Levels on the Student *Evaluation Test* Report and the Student *Diagnostic Test* Report.

   - **To fill in the Reading Skills Order of Importance Chart** — If a fifth-grade student has a reading level in the 4-1 to 4-3 range, look at the column for *Instructional Reading Level* 4-1 to 4-3 on The Importance of Reading Skills as Determined by *Instructional Reading Levels* on page 83. You'll see that Sounds-Letters: Vowels has some importance; Vocabulary in Context and Word Part Clues have high importance; and Skimming and Scanning has some importance. You'll find criterion scores on page 84.

   - **To fill in the Reading Comprehension Skills and Strategies Chart** — If a student scores 15 on the Inferential Comprehension part of the Reading Comprehension Test, look at the line for Inferential Comprehension on the Cut Score Criteria for the grade 5 Test on page 84. You'll see that a score of 15 is in the Developing Level, so you mark *Developing* in the space for Inferential Comprehension.

   - **To fill in the Criterion Scores on the Student *Diagnostic Test* Report** — If a student scores 16 on the Vocabulary in Context Test, look at the line for Vocabulary in Context on the Cut Score Criteria for the grade 5 Test on page 84. You'll see that a score of 16 is in the Developing Level, so mark *Developing* under Criterion Score in the space for Vocabulary in Context on the Student *Diagnostic Test* Report.

   - **To fill in the Action Plan** — Look at the Action Plans for the grade 5 test beginning on page 85 in the Appendix. When you have confirmed your student's *Instructional Reading Level,* find the Action Plan for that *Instructional Reading Level* here and copy or fill in the information on the Student *Evaluation Test* Report Blackline Master.

3. When the student reports are complete, you can roll the student information up into a Class *Evaluation Test* Report and a Class *Diagnostic Test* Report, found on pages 74 and 76 in the Appendix.

Student *Evaluation Test* Report Blackline Master

RIGBY READS Reading Evaluation and Diagnostic System

Name _____ Grade _____

Teacher _____ Date Tested _____

Test Administered: Grade _____ Form _____

Functional Reading Levels

Instructional Reading Level	Independent Reading Level

Reading Skills Order of Importance

High Importance	
Some Importance	
Low Importance	

Reading Comprehension Skills and Strategies

Reading Skills and Strategies	Criterion Score
Literal Comprehension	
Inferential Comprehension	
Critical Comprehension	

Action Plan

For Recommended Reading List:
WEB www.harcourtachieve.com/READS · **PHONE** 1-800-531-5015 · **FAX** 1-800-699-9458

Student *Diagnostic Test* Report Blackline Master

RIGBY READS Reading Evaluation and Diagnostic System

Name _____ Grade _____

Teacher _____ Date Tested _____

Test Administered: Grade _____ Form _____

Functional Reading Levels

Instructional Reading Level	Independent Reading Level

Reading Skills in Order of Importance

Importance	Reading Skill/Strategy	Criterion Score
High		
Some		
Low		

Criterion Scores

	Number Possible	Number Correct	Criterion Score
Sounds-Letters: Consonants Total			
Beginning Consonants			
Ending Consonants			
Sounds-Letters: Vowels Total			
Short Vowels			
Long Vowels			
Digraphs/Diphthongs			

	Number Possible	Number Correct	Criterion Score
Word Part Clues Total			
Inflections/Prefixes			
Vocabulary in Context Total			
Reading Comprehension Total			
Literal			
Inferential			
Critical			

For Recommended Reading List:
WEB www.harcourtachieve.com/READS · **PHONE** 1-800-531-5015 · **FAX** 1-800-699-9458

Scoring Service

Student Answer Sheets (*Evaluation* and *Diagnostic Tests* for Grades 4–8)

The scoring service scans the Answer Sheets and scores them for you. This service is only available for customers who have prepaid for this scoring service, as indicated by the green color of the Answer Sheets. The scoring service will only process the green Answer Sheets.

If you are interested in ordering the scoring service or have any questions, please call 1-800-531-5015.

1. All Student Answer Sheets should be collected at the conclusion of the test. (Return test booklets to the school testing coordinator to maintain the integrity of the test results.)

2. Group all Student Answer Sheets by class.

3. Place Student Answer Sheets faceup and in the same direction. It is not necessary to alphabetize the Answer Sheets.

4. Completely fill out and bubble in the appropriate data on one Teacher Header Sheet. **There must be one Teacher Header Sheet for each class or group of students tested.**

5. Place the completed Teacher Header Sheet on top of the Student Answer Sheets facing in the same direction.

6. Place the class set of Student Answer Sheets and the accompanying Teacher Header Sheet in the envelope included with each package of Answer Sheets. Do not use rubber bands or paper clips.

7. Each envelope must contain Answer Sheets for the same test level and test form as indicated on the accompanying Teacher Header Sheet.

8. With each package of Answer Sheets is a READS Summary Sheet. Please complete one READS Summary Sheet and include it with each order that is to be scored.

9. The READS school testing coordinator should gather all Answer Sheet envelopes and place all the envelopes from the school into a box.

10. Send all completed documents to:

    RIGBY READS Scoring Center
    TASA, Inc.
    4 Hardscrabble Heights
    Brewster, New York 10509

Proper completion and packaging of Answer Sheets, Teacher Header Sheets and Summary Sheets will ensure that your results will be returned within three weeks of our receipt of your documents.

Overview of the Report Forms

Rigby READS provides a variety of reports. The Student *Evaluation Test* Report, Class *Evaluation Test* Report, Student *Diagnostic Test* Report, Class *Diagnostic Test* Report, Student Yearly Progress Report, and Class Yearly Progress Report are explained in detail on pages 32–43. Blackline masters of those reports and A Letter Home are available on pages 73–81 of this Teacher's Manual as well as online and through the scoring service.

A Letter Home is available in English and Spanish. Space is provided on the letter to inform parents and caregivers of the student's *Independent* and *Instructional Reading Levels*. There are suggestions for reading at home with the student. You may attach to the letter a list of books at the student's *Independent Reading Level* that you'll find at www.harcourtachieve.com/READS. (Students who have an *Instructional Reading Level* of Early Readiness or Kindergarten will not have an *Independent Reading Level* and therefore will not have a list of suggested books.)

The remaining reports are available online or through the scoring service only. They include:

Student Test Status. This report tells you when a student has completed a test. If the student has not completed the test, the report states the cause of the incomplete test.

Grade Proficiency Report. This report shows how many students in a given grade are reading above grade level, on grade level, or below grade level. It also contains a summary of the *Instructional* and *Independent Reading Levels* for the students in each grade.

School Proficiency Report. This report rolls up the Grade Proficiency Reports from all grade levels. This report is useful for an administrator who needs to compare the reading proficiency of students at various grade levels.

District Proficiency Report. This report rolls up the School Proficiency Reports from all schools in the district. It shows how many students in each school are reading above grade level, on grade level, or below grade level. It also contains a summary of the *Instructional* and *Independent Reading Levels* for each school by grade.

Student *Evaluation Test* Report

Who should see this report?
This report should be very helpful to any teacher or specialist who needs specific information for helping an individual student learn to read.

What is the focus of this report?
This report is based on each student's performance on the *Rigby READS Evaluation Test*. The information is especially valuable if you want to determine a student's *Instructional* and *Independent Reading Levels* so that specific books can be identified that will help the student have success as a reader.

The reading skills and strategies identified on the report form are based on the student's *Instructional Reading Level*. These skills and strategies have been determined by reviewing thousands of students' score reports when students took both reading comprehension and reading skills tests. The reading skills and strategies listed as *High Importance, Some Importance,* and *Low Importance* are empirically based judgments derived from data on all of these students.

When would this report be used?
This report is most valuable as you are planning instruction. However, it is also useful at the end of an instructional period to determine reading growth.

How does this report lead to action?
The Action Plan, beginning on page 85, pulls together all of the analysis and provides you with a useful instructional plan for each student.

What does the report tell you?

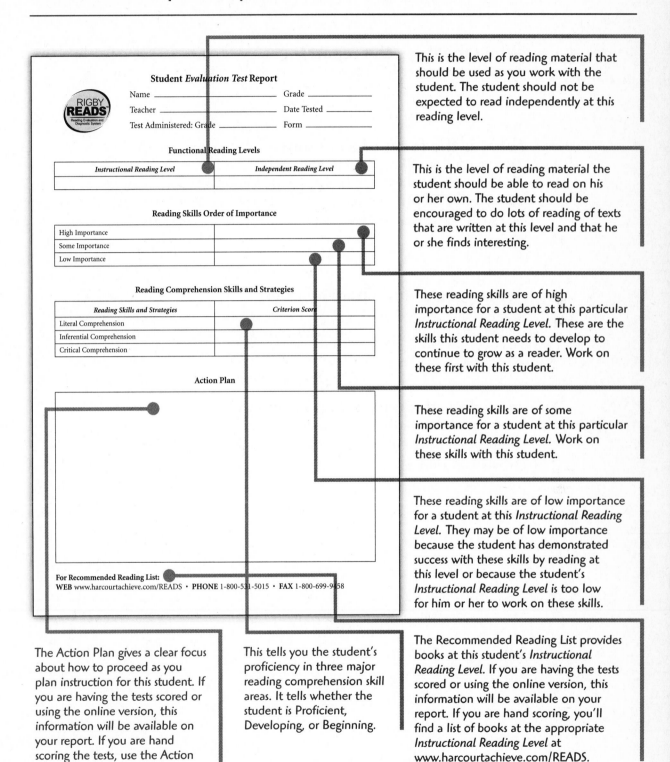

Student *Evaluation Test* Report

RIGBY **READS**
Reading Evaluation and Diagnostic System

Name _____ Grade _____
Teacher _____ Date Tested _____
Test Administered: Grade _____ Form _____

Functional Reading Levels

Instructional Reading Level	Independent Reading Level

Reading Skills Order of Importance

High Importance	
Some Importance	
Low Importance	

Reading Comprehension Skills and Strategies

Reading Skills and Strategies	Criterion Score
Literal Comprehension	
Inferential Comprehension	
Critical Comprehension	

Action Plan

For Recommended Reading List:
WEB www.harcourtachieve.com/READS • PHONE 1-800-531-5015 • FAX 1-800-699-9458

This is the level of reading material that should be used as you work with the student. The student should not be expected to read independently at this reading level.

This is the level of reading material the student should be able to read on his or her own. The student should be encouraged to do lots of reading of texts that are written at this level and that he or she finds interesting.

These reading skills are of high importance for a student at this particular *Instructional Reading Level.* These are the skills this student needs to develop to continue to grow as a reader. Work on these first with this student.

These reading skills are of some importance for a student at this particular *Instructional Reading Level.* Work on these skills with this student.

These reading skills are of low importance for a student at this *Instructional Reading Level.* They may be of low importance because the student has demonstrated success with these skills by reading at this level or because the student's *Instructional Reading Level* is too low for him or her to work on these skills.

The Action Plan gives a clear focus about how to proceed as you plan instruction for this student. If you are having the tests scored or using the online version, this information will be available on your report. If you are hand scoring the tests, use the Action Plan information beginning on page 85 in the Appendix.

This tells you the student's proficiency in three major reading comprehension skill areas. It tells whether the student is Proficient, Developing, or Beginning.

The Recommended Reading List provides books at this student's *Instructional Reading Level.* If you are having the tests scored or using the online version, this information will be available on your report. If you are hand scoring, you'll find a list of books at the appropriate *Instructional Reading Level* at www.harcourtachieve.com/READS.

Class *Evaluation Test* Report

Who should see this report?
Classroom teachers and administrators should see this report.

What is the focus of this report?
The summary provides an excellent synopsis of a class's reading levels by showing both the number and percent of students at various reading levels. This report is available for both Form A and Form B of the *Rigby READS* test and so can determine progress across a semester or a school year.

When would this report be used?
This report is valuable as instruction is being planned as well as at the end of an instructional period to determine reading growth.

How does this report lead to action?
The information provides an excellent means for grouping students in appropriately leveled reading groups and for developing instructional plans for an entire class.

What does the report tell you?

Class *Evaluation Test* Report

RIGBY
READS
Reading Evaluation and
Diagnostic System

Name _____   Grade _____

Teacher _____   Date Tested _____

Test Administered: Grade _____   Form _____

Evaluation Test Results Summary

Reading Level	Below Grade Level	On Grade Level	Above Grade Level
Number of Students			

> This chart shows how many students are reading below, on, or above grade level.

Reading Level	2-4 minus	3-1 to 3-2	3-3	4-1 to 4-3	5-1 to 5-3	6-1 to 6-2	7 plus
Instructional Number of Students							
Percent of Class							
Independent Number of Students							
Percent of Class							

> This is a summary of the *Instructional* and *Independent Reading Levels* for the students in your class. This summary information can help you determine the makeup of reading groups.

Student	Instructional Reading Level	Independent Reading Level

> This is list of students and their *Instructional* and *Independent Reading Levels*.

Student *Diagnostic Test* Report

Who should see this report?

This report will help any teacher or reading specialist who needs specific information regarding a student's reading levels as well as the student's performance on the skills and strategies of reading. The information can form the basis for an individual prescriptive plan.

What is the focus of this report?

This report is based on a student's performance on the *Rigby READS Diagnostic Test*. The information is especially valuable if you want to determine each student's *Instructional* and *Independent Reading Levels* so that specific books can be identified that will help the student have success as a reader. This report also provides specific information about each student's performance on tests of reading skills and strategies.

When would this report be used?

This report is most valuable as instruction is being planned. However, it is also useful at the end of an instructional period to determine reading growth.

How does this report lead to action?

This report provides a comprehensive summary of a student's functional reading levels so that specific books and stories can be selected for both instruction and independent reading. The skills and strategies analysis provides you with a focused and detailed instructional plan.

What does the report tell you?

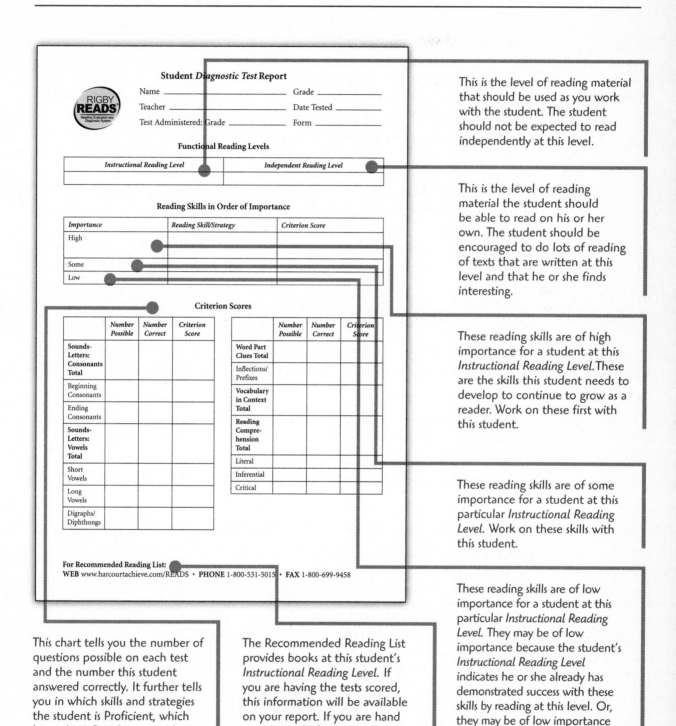

Student *Diagnostic Test* Report

RIGBY READS
Reading Evaluation and Diagnostic System

Name _____ Grade _____

Teacher _____ Date Tested _____

Test Administered: Grade _____ Form _____

Functional Reading Levels

Instructional Reading Level	Independent Reading Level

Reading Skills in Order of Importance

Importance	Reading Skill/Strategy	Criterion Score
High		
Some		
Low		

Criterion Scores

	Number Possible	Number Correct	Criterion Score
Sounds-Letters: Consonants Total			
Beginning Consonants			
Ending Consonants			
Sounds-Letters: Vowels Total			
Short Vowels			
Long Vowels			
Digraphs/ Diphthongs			

	Number Possible	Number Correct	Criterion Score
Word Part Clues Total			
Inflections/ Prefixes			
Vocabulary in Context Total			
Reading Comprehension Total			
Literal			
Inferential			
Critical			

For Recommended Reading List:
WEB www.harcourtachieve.com/READS • **PHONE** 1-800-531-5015 • **FAX** 1-800-699-9458

This is the level of reading material that should be used as you work with the student. The student should not be expected to read independently at this level.

This is the level of reading material the student should be able to read on his or her own. The student should be encouraged to do lots of reading of texts that are written at this level and that he or she finds interesting.

These reading skills are of high importance for a student at this *Instructional Reading Level.* These are the skills this student needs to develop to continue to grow as a reader. Work on these first with this student.

These reading skills are of some importance for a student at this particular *Instructional Reading Level.* Work on these skills with this student.

This chart tells you the number of questions possible on each test and the number this student answered correctly. It further tells you in which skills and strategies the student is Proficient, which he or she is Developing, and which skills he or she is just Beginning to need.

The Recommended Reading List provides books at this student's *Instructional Reading Level.* If you are having the tests scored, this information will be available on your report. If you are hand scoring, you'll find a list of books at the appropriate *Instructional Reading Level* at www.harcourtachieve.com/READS.

These reading skills are of low importance for a student at this particular *Instructional Reading Level.* They may be of low importance because the student's *Instructional Reading Level* indicates he or she already has demonstrated success with these skills by reading at this level. Or, they may be of low importance because the student's *Instructional Reading Level* is too low for him or her to work on these skills.

Class *Diagnostic Test* Report

Who should see this report?

Both classroom teachers and administrators should see this report. The report is especially useful to a classroom teacher who needs an overview of the number and percent of the students at various reading levels and the numbers and percents of students at the proficient, developing, and beginning levels regarding specific reading skills and strategies.

What is the focus of this report?

This report is a comprehensive diagnostic report of the reading levels and reading skills performance for all of the students in a class. The reading levels are based on each student's performance on the *Rigby READS Diagnostic Test*. The information is especially valuable for a teacher who wants a single list of the students' *Instructional* and *Independent Reading Levels* so specific books can be identified that will help students have success as a reader.

The reading skills and strategies performance levels are indicated by whether each student scored at a *Proficient, Developing,* or *Beginning* level.

When would this report be used?

This report is valuable as instruction is being planned as well as at the end of an instructional period to determine reading growth.

How does this report lead to action?

The report provides the reading level and the reading skill performance of every student in the class. The summary information is presented in a way that allows you to see at a glance how many students are reading at various *Instructional* and *Independent Reading Levels*. This information can be used to select books and as a guide to focusing on needed reading skill and strategy instruction. Specific teaching suggestions for the skills are included in Chapter 4 of this manual. Those suggestions coupled with the information in this Class *Diagnostic Test* Report provide an excellent means to develop instructional plans for an entire class.

What does the report tell you?

Class *Diagnostic Test* Report

RIGBY
READS
Reading Evaluation and
Diagnostic System

Name _____ Grade _____

Teacher _____ Date Tested _____

Test Administered: Grade _____ Form _____

***Diagnostic Test* Results Summary**

Reading Level	Below Grade Level	On Grade Level	Above Grade Level
Number of Students			

Reading Level or Reading Skill	2-4 minus	3-1 to 3-2	3-3	4-1 to 4-3	5-1 to 5-3	6-1 to 6-2	7 plus
Instructional Level Number of Students							
Percent of Class							
Independent Level Number of Students							
Percent of Class							

	Proficient	Developing	Beginning
Sounds-Letters: Consonants Number of Students			
Percent of Class			
Sounds-Letters: Vowels Number of Students			
Percent of Class			
Word Part Clues Number of Students			
Percent of Class			
Vocabulary Number of Students			
Percent of Class			
Comprehension Number of Students			
Percent of Class			

This chart shows how many students are reading below, on, or above grade level.

This is a summary of the *Instructional* and *Independent Reading Levels* for the students in your class. This summary information can help you determine the makeup of reading groups.

This is a list of the number and percent of students who are Proficient, Developing, and Beginning in the skills tested on the *Rigby READS Diagnostic Test*. This is valuable information for time management in planning whole-class and small-group instruction on specific skills.

Student Names	Functional Reading Levels		Performance on Reading Skills and Strategies							
	Instructional Reading Level	Independent Reading Level	Sounds-Letters Consonants	Sounds-Letters Vowels	Word Part Clues	Vocabulary	Comprehension			
							Literal	Inferential	Critical	

This chart provides a great deal of information.

- It is a list of students and their *Instructional* and *Independent Reading Levels.*

- It is a summary of the suggested reading skills of importance for your students. This summary can help you plan instruction to target individual needs.

Student Yearly Progress Report

Who should see this report?

This report is designed primarily for the classroom teacher or specialist to assess individual students' growth in reading comprehension over a period of time, typically a school year.

Teachers could also show this report to parents as an illustration of their child's progress during the year. However, it is recommended that the report be used only in face-to-face meetings, not sent home. The information conveyed on the report would be very difficult for parents to interpret meaningfully without professional guidance by the teacher.

What is the focus of this report?

The report graphs individual students' achievement in reading comprehension at different points in a school year. This report uses a *scaled score*, which is a "growth" score that permits comparisons between different test forms. Raw scores cannot be appropriately used for such comparisons because the individual test questions differ between tests.

The graph displays a student's Reading Comprehension scaled score for the times within a school year that READS was administered. The graph indicates whether the student's achievement has improved during the year and, if so, the rate of improvement.

Note that if you are using READS Online, the Student Yearly Progress Report graph will appear on screen as a bar graph. However, the report will print out as a line graph.

When would this report be used?

This report is useful at the end of the school year to assess the adequate yearly progress (AYP) made by an individual student in reading comprehension. It would also be a valuable document for the student's teacher at the beginning of the following school year as a summary of the amount of growth shown the previous year and as an indicator of the appropriate level to begin reading instruction for that student.

How does this report lead to action?

This report, when combined with those of other students in the class (see **Class Yearly Progress Report**), can be a useful "wrap-up" of students' progress—either those in an intact classroom or in special remedial or enrichment situations.

What does the report tell you?

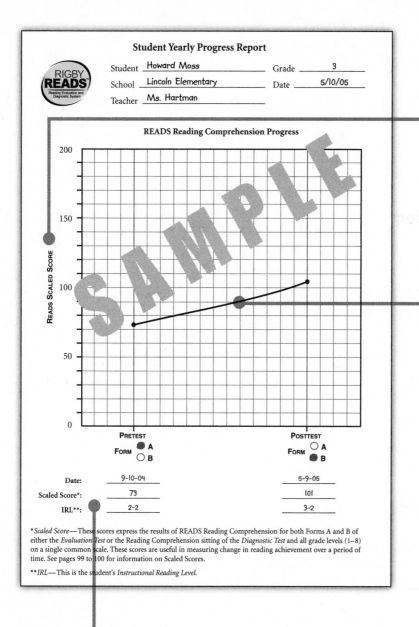

Student Yearly Progress Report

Student __Howard Moss__ Grade __3__
School __Lincoln Elementary__ Date __5/10/05__
Teacher __Ms. Hartman__

READS Reading Comprehension Progress

SAMPLE

	PRETEST	POSTTEST
	FORM ●A ○B	FORM ○A ●B
Date:	9-10-04	5-9-05
Scaled Score*:	73	101
IRL**:	2-2	3-2

*Scaled Score—These scores express the results of READS Reading Comprehension for both Forms A and B of either the *Evaluation Test* or the Reading Comprehension sitting of the *Diagnostic Test* and all grade levels (1–8) on a single common scale. These scores are useful in measuring change in reading achievement over a period of time. See pages 99 to 100 for information on Scaled Scores.

**IRL—This is the student's *Instructional Reading Level*.

The graphs of student Reading Comprehension scores are in terms of scaled scores, which permit an assessment of achievement change over time regardless of form or level of the test. Scaled scores for READS range from 1 through 200.

The plotted line shows the progress across testing periods for a particular student. If two READS tests were administered in this school year, this plot is a straight line connecting the pretest and posttest scaled scores. Each Student Yearly Progress Report will, of course, be different.

Information provided in this section will be the test dates and the obtained scaled score and IRL for each test administration.

Class Yearly Progress Report

Who should see this report?

This report is designed primarily for the classroom teacher or specialist to assess a classroom-sized group of students' growth in reading comprehension over a period of time, typically a school year.

What is the focus of this report?

The report shows the reading comprehension achievement of classroom-sized groups of students at different points in a school year. Individual students' scores are shown for each test, and an average score for the group is displayed. The score metric used for this report is a *scaled score*, which is a "growth" score that permits comparisons between different test forms and levels. Raw scores cannot be appropriately used for such comparisons because the individual test questions differ between tests.

The graph displays each student's Reading Comprehension scaled scores for the two times within a school year that READS was administered. The graph indicates the amount of progress shown by each *individual* student as well as the average growth shown by the *group* during the year.

The report arranges all students into three groups—those whose pretest *Instructional Reading Level* (IRL) was above grade placement, those whose IRL was "on-grade," and those with pretest IRLs below grade placement.

When would this report be used?

This report is useful at the end of the school year to assess the progress made by a group of students in reading comprehension during the year. The report can help classroom teachers document adequate yearly progress (AYP) for both individual students and class groups.

How does this report lead to action?

This report is a useful "wrap-up" of students' progress—either those in an intact classroom or in groups of students in special remedial or enrichment situations. It can be useful to teachers, specialists, or administrators in planning student-grouping approaches for the subsequent school year.

What does the report tell you?

Class Yearly Progress Report

RIGBY **READS**
Reading Evaluation and
Diagnostic System

School **Lincoln Elementary** Grade **3**

Teacher **Ms. Hartman** School Year **2004-2005**

READS Reading Comprehension Progress by Student

		READS Test Dates		READS Scaled Scores*			
	Student	Pre	Post	Pre	Post	Gain	SS Growth
Above-Level Readers	Bob Reed	9/10/04	5/03/05	103	163	60	
	Max Smith	9/10/04	5/03/05	98	149	51	
	Alicia Karas	9/10/04	5/03/05	99	146	47	
	Bess Larkin	11/16/04	5/03/05	87	127	40	
On-Level Readers	Linda Healy	9/10/04	5/03/05		3	4	
	Mike Barth	9/10/04	5/	75	113	40	
	Lisa Haley	2/06/	/0	76		32	
	Howard Moss	9/10/04	/0		101	28	
	Jana Elson	/04	5/ /05	71	80	9	
Below-Level Readers	Wil /04		5/03/05	56	106	50	
	Nelson M ks	9/10/04	5/03/05	62	101	39	
	Sue Simpson	9/10/04	5/07/05	60	89	29	
	Cathy Carson	9/10/04	5/03/05	56	76	20	
	Patsy Dunn	9/10/04	5/03/05	48	52	4	
	Suzie Ratson	9/11/04	5/03/05	37	36	-1	
	Class Average			72	105	30	

Scaled Score—These scores express the results of READS Reading Comprehension for both Forms A and B of
either the *Evaluation Test* or the Reading Comprehension sitting of the *Diagnostic Test* and all grade levels (1–8)
on a single common scale. These scores are useful in measuring change in reading achievement over a period of
time. See pages 99 to 100 for information on Scaled Scores. A student with negative growth in reading
achievement will not have a bar graph in the right column.

Students in the class are grouped according to their pretest *Instructional Reading Level* (IRL). "On-Level Readers" are those with pretest IRLs corresponding to their grade placement. Within each of the three groups, students are sequenced high to low according to their **gain** in Reading Comprehension from pretest to posttest.

The graphs of student Reading Comprehension scores are in terms of scaled scores, which permit an assessment of achievement change over time regardless of form or level of the test. Scaled scores for READS range from 1 through 200.

This section of the report shows each student's Pretest and Posttest Reading Comprehension scaled score, the gain in scaled scores (SS) from pretest to posttest, and a graphic representation of this gain.

The SS Growth plot for each student is the amount of scaled score change from pretest to posttest.

The READS pretest (Form A) and posttest (Form B) dates of test administration are shown for each student. Since the test is group-administered, the test dates will typically be the same for most students in the class.

This section of the report summarizes the pretest, posttest, and gain scores for all students shown on the report. It shows the mean scores for the class, along with a graph of the mean scaled-score growth.

Chapter 4
Using the Test Results

Interpreting the test results of *Rigby READS* involves looking at the specifics of each student's *Instructional Reading Level* and *Skills of Importance* on both the *Evaluation* and *Diagnostic Tests*. It also means checking carefully how the student performed on the various reading skills tests on the *Diagnostic Test*.

It is important to consider more than just the scores on specific tests. The following general guidelines provide a process that should help as you review each student's performance on both the *Evaluation* and *Diagnostic Tests*.

General Guidelines

- **Begin with a general picture, then go on to more specific considerations.**

  Before assessing performance on specific tests and objectives, try to get an overall picture of your student's achievement by examining his or her *Instructional Reading Level*. Next, examine the skills tests that are most important for a student with that particular *Instructional Reading Level*.

  If your student's reading test scores from previous years are available, you can compare them to see how he or she has performed. Knowing that a student has had difficulty in learning to read for some time will alert you to the fact that he or she will probably need concentrated help in order to overcome certain persistent problems.

  In addition, a comparison of your student's overall reading performance with performance in other curriculum areas such as mathematics and oral and written language can be useful in deciding whether one area needs more instructional emphasis than another. Such comparisons also tell you if reading is the major problem your student is encountering or whether the student is having problems in several subject areas.

- **Don't overemphasize small differences.**

  While tests such as *Rigby READS* are a good source of information, like any other measuring instrument, they are not perfect. If the tests were re-administered, or if another form of the tests were given, most students' raw scores would be slightly different. Small differences between a student's scores in different areas are best treated as random fluctuation.

■ **Remember that every student can learn more.**

A wide range of individual differences can be found in virtually every classroom. No matter how high or low a student's performance is, he or she can become a better reader. This principle is the key to individualizing an educational program. *Rigby READS* is designed to assist you in planning a course of instruction for each student. The *Instructional Reading Level* is the key to matching students with leveled readers for reading instruction to ensure success.

■ *Rigby READS* **tests are criterion-referenced tests.**

Much has been written about the relative merits of norm-referenced and criterion-referenced interpretation of test scores. Both kinds of interpretation are useful and, when possible, both should be used. However, the *Rigby READS* tests are based on extensive tryouts and research that provide criterion-referenced interpretations that are useful for planning instruction and assessing growth.

Criterion-referenced interpretations:
— ask whether a student can meet a specific standard.
— are crucial in matching students with books in which they can experience success and growth.
— provide specific suggestions for instructional decision-making. Such interpretations might also be called "instructional-referenced" interpretations. Furthermore, since this type of interpretation most often takes place at the standard or objective level, it can be called a "standard-referenced" or "objective-referenced" interpretation.

■ **Interrelate the different areas.**

When you interpret a student's performance, it is very important to interrelate the results from different reading strategy or skill areas. While reading can be arbitrarily divided into the strategy or skill areas corresponding to tests, each is part of an integrated total picture.

■ **Consider the student's interests and attitude.**

Most of the teaching suggestions provided in curriculum materials are aimed at skill or cognitive development. Each student's background and interests should also be taken into account when interpreting test results and planning instruction for two reasons:
— The development of reading interests is an important objective in its own right.
— Each student's interests, based on his or her background experiences, affect your instructional planning for reading growth.

Your students can be better motivated with stories and books that are familiar and enjoyable. At the same time, make special efforts to develop your students' experiential background in order to broaden their reading interests.

■ **Use the test results for instructional planning.**

The interpretation of *Rigby READS* test results should focus on instructional planning. Whenever results for a student or a class are being reviewed, ask questions such as the following:

— What do the results suggest about *what* I should teach?
— What do the results suggest about *how* I should teach?
— Which skills should be *reviewed* for the class? for individual students?
— Which skills should be *taught* next in the instructional sequence for the class? for individual students?

■ **Plan for follow-up evaluation.**

The administration of the *Rigby READS Evaluation* or *Diagnostic Tests* serves as an assessment point in an ongoing instructional program. Provide continuous follow-up evaluation to determine what skills your students have learned, what progress has been made, and where to go next. Many curriculum materials include evaluations that can be used on a daily or weekly basis. For more comprehensive follow-up evaluation over a longer period of time, you can administer an alternate form of the *Rigby READS Evaluation* or *Diagnostic Tests*.

Factors Affecting Achievement

Keep several issues in mind when interpreting test performance.

■ **Personal Factors:**
— Does the student have any physical disabilities (hearing loss, vision problems, etc.)?
— What is the student's school attendance record?
— Does the student receive help with schoolwork at home?
— Is a different language spoken at home than at school?
— Is the student's experiential background different from that of other students?
— What other conditions might the student have been reacting to on the day he or she was tested?

■ **School Factors:**
— Does the student appear interested in schoolwork?
— Is the student substantially overage or underage for the grade?
— Is the student comfortable in the school environment?
— Has the student changed schools frequently?
— Is sufficient time allotted to the subjects that present the greatest difficulty for the student?
— What are the student's study and work habits?
— Are realistic expectations being set for the student?

Test scores should be viewed as just one type of information about a student. Teacher observation; daily work samples; the student's background, physical and mental factors; and school factors should all be part of a comprehensive evaluation for each student.

Teaching Reading Comprehension

Factors to Consider When Interpreting Student Performance

The primary factor to consider when interpreting your students' performance on the Reading Comprehension Test is the *Instructional Reading Level*. In addition to determining the level of instructional reading materials, a student's *Instructional Reading Level* indicates which of the reading skills are of *High, Some*, or *Low Importance* when planning for instruction.

Tips for Teaching Reading Comprehension

When the goal of instruction is to increase reading comprehension, provide your students with materials that they can read successfully. Have available a supply of interesting materials at both your students' *Instructional* and *Independent Reading Levels*. The following recommendations are divided into five areas that are aimed at improving your students' reading comprehension:

- Establishing purposes for reading

- Building on interests

- Building background knowledge

- Enhancing motivation

- Providing follow-up and application

Instruction in reading comprehension encompasses combinations of all five of these areas.

- **Establishing Purposes for Reading.** Students should have a purpose for reading each selection. A student who reads for a specified purpose is actively engaged in trying to make sense of what is being read. You can help your students learn to develop purposes for reading by:
    - ensuring that your students always have a purpose for reading. At first a purpose is established through discussions with your students; then your students generate a purpose on their own. It is important that your students learn to internalize the process of establishing a purpose for reading.
    - initially providing your students with purposes for reading by posing questions before reading, such as, "Let's read this story to find out why. . . ."

— capitalizing on your students' curiosity. This is often accomplished when you read or tell your students the first part of a story and encourage them to read to see what happens next.

- **Building on Interests.** Your students' reading interests are closely related to their purposes for reading. You can use these interests to improve reading comprehension by:
  - learning what your students' interests are.
  - bringing reading materials to class that relate to your students' interests.
  - expressing a desire to share in your students' interests with them.
  - talking with your students about their interests and activities and sharing with them special interests and activities of your own.

- **Building Background Knowledge.** You can enhance your students' understanding by building background knowledge before they read. Build background knowledge for reading by:
  - using community resources to bring in different kinds of materials and speakers to talk with your students. Organize field trips to places in the community.
  - introducing new words and concepts before your students encounter them in a story.
  - identifying key concepts in a selection to be read and using these as a focus for a class discussion.
  - providing your students with some ideas about why an author might have written a particular story. Ask them why they think the author wrote the story.

- **Enhancing Motivation.** Motivation is based on interests, and increases when a specific purpose for reading has been established. Other ways to increase motivation include:
  - relating the story to events in your students' lives.
  - discussing pictures and story titles emphasizing the usefulness of what is to be read. For example, "After we read this article on how to build an ant farm, we will be able to start one in our classroom. Be sure you read each step carefully so you'll know how to do it."

- **Providing Follow-up and Application.** In addition to answering questions about what has been read, reading comprehension also includes the use and application of what has been read. You can increase your students' comprehension by planning reading instruction to include a wide variety of follow-up and application activities. These should be related to the purposes for reading, which have been established prior to reading the selection. These activities might include:
  - making a map of the locations of events in a story.
  - putting on a puppet show or Readers' Theatre based on a story.
  - creating a different story ending.

Teaching Specific Comprehension Skills and Strategies

Many books and articles are written about the teaching of reading comprehension skills and strategies. Several of these are included in the references beginning on page 101 in the Appendix. The following is an overview of some approaches to teaching reading comprehension. There are three types of reasoning that you can promote with your students:

- Reading to identify and remember facts and details

- Reading to understand main ideas and generalizations

- Reading to understand the relationships between ideas by using such techniques as sequence and enumeration, cause and effect, and comparing and contrasting

Each area of reasoning is further defined and illustrated below.

- **Identifying and Remembering Facts and Details**

    A reader identifies facts and details because he or she needs the information for a specific purpose. Facts and details are also needed to develop major ideas and generalizations. The facts or details may be specifically stated or inferred, and often their relevance or validity needs to be evaluated. When encouraging your students to focus on facts and details, remember that there must be a specific purpose for which the facts and details are needed. In addition, your students need some organizational schema with which to relate the facts and details; this schema should develop from their purpose for reading.

    — Following directions
    Following directions is an instance when your students need to identify and remember facts and details. You can help your students with this task by giving categories for remembering information, such as, "things to watch for."

    — Reporting facts and details
    Your students often want to share what they have read. Younger students can draw a picture of a story event or characters, or a map depicting a story setting. Older students can make models of story characters out of clay or other materials or write a class newspaper.

    — Validating and supporting ideas
    A very common need of any reader is to validate his or her ideas. You can use questioning as one strategy to ask your students to verify what they have read. Questions such as, "How do you know that?" or "What makes you think that?" can promote discussion and emphasize identifying the facts and details to support ideas.

— Categorizing facts and details

There are times when your students might be reading to find out what it might be like to live in another place or time. When reading for such a purpose, you can help your students categorize facts and details by providing one or two categories for noting the information.

— Defining descriptive words

You can help your students describe story characters, settings, and events by discussing adjectives, phrases, and other descriptive words from the story.

■ Understanding Main Ideas and Generalizations

Main ideas and generalizations are defined by the relationship of various pieces of information to the rest of the information in a story or article. Main ideas and generalizations often need to be inferred by the reader from what the author has written.

— Main ideas and generalizations

A student needs to learn that main ideas and generalizations develop from facts and details. You can encourage this learning when you read to your students and talk with them about the story characters, the story setting, and the events in a story. Structure your discussions so that a student identifies the facts and details that give rise to main ideas and generalizations or vice versa.

— Character development

Students often become very interested in the characters they are reading about. After they are finished reading, they might want to pretend to be these characters. Puppets and role playing are useful ways to allow students to portray the characters they have been reading about.

— Moods and settings

Sometimes your students are reading to find out what it would be like to live in a particular place. Ask your students to suggest one word that would describe that place to see whether they have captured the generalization.

— Describing events

The most common reasons for reading a story are to enjoy it and to find out what happened. There are many ways to help your students think about the events in a story. Oral or written retelling, artwork, drama, and even music activities are useful ways to encourage a student to describe to others an event in a story.

■ Understanding Relationships

When your students read to understand the relationships among facts, main ideas, and generalizations, they are searching for an overall organization of the material. The ability to identify the relationships between ideas is not necessarily dependent upon initially recognizing the facts. Sometimes the relationships between generalizations can help. You might ask, "Was it important that things happened in exactly that order?" or "What would have happened if _____ didn't happen first?" Through such discussion and questions you are not only able to focus your students' attention on the sequence, but also to review the sequence of events critically.

— Cause and effect

Causal relationships are a sequence with a cause and its effect, which, in turn, becomes the cause of still another effect. In teaching this aspect of comprehension, your aim is to make your students aware that frequently one event does not just follow another, but may stem from a previous event or condition. As young readers become aware of this kind of relationship, their reasoning leads them to look back from an action for its cause.

— Comparing and contrasting

In comparing, the similarities between two or more things or ideas are pointed out. In contrasting, differences are pointed out. When making a list of ways in which two story characters are alike or different, focus your students' attention on comparing and contrasting. In addition, drawings, which often allow a student to indicate even subtle differences, can be used instead of lists.

Teaching Phonics

Factors to Consider When Interpreting Student Performance

When interpreting each student's performance on the *Rigby READS* Sounds-Letters: Vowels and Sounds-Letters: Consonants Tests, consider your student's *Instructional Reading Level*. For example, a student who has an *Instructional Reading Level* in the grade 5 range should not have great emphasis placed on sound-letter matching. However, a student with an *Instructional Reading Level* in the grade 2 range will probably need instruction on sound-letter matching. The Student *Diagnostic Test* Report will help you determine the type of instructional program appropriate for each student.

Tips for Teaching Sound-Letter Matching

Keep the following general principles in mind when teaching sound-letter matching:

- Use the materials for teaching phonics at or below the student's *Independent Reading Level*, which is slightly below the student's *Instructional Reading Level*.

- Relationships between sounds and letters are usually taught and learned more effectively in the context of words and text.

- Your students should not be expected to sound out a word that is not in their oral vocabulary.

- Avoid identifying a sound as a combination of letters. For example, instead of saying the *"s-h" sound*, emphasize that the letters stand for *one* sound, as in *sh*are, *sh*ip, or *sh*ow.

- Introduce phonic elements one at a time. Emphasize those that appear in your students' reading materials and that will further their independence as readers. Provide instruction and practice with each element.

- Avoid correcting speech problems during phonic instruction.

- Comprehension should be the focus of instruction when teaching word recognition skills so that your students will use their knowledge as aids in the recognition and understanding of printed words.

To avoid repetitive drill that can create negative attitudes toward reading, try some of the following activities to help your students practice and apply their phonics skills.

- Play the game "I Spy" with your students. Each student takes a turn spying an object that begins with a particular sound. Modify the game by using medial or final sounds.

- Have pairs of students look through catalogs or magazines for pictures of items that begin or end with specific sounds. Have them cut out each picture, paste it on paper, and write the word that matches the picture beside it.

- Divide the class into two teams. The first player on Team A says a word, such as *shout*. The first player on Team B must say a word that begins with the last sound—in this case, /t/—and use that word in a sentence. The game continues as teams alternate. Vary the game by changing the types of matches required.

- Give your students opportunities to practice vowel substitutions. Lists such as the following could be presented:

t_____n	fl_____p	h__m
t_____n	fl_____p	h__m
t_____n	fl_____p	h__m
t_____n	fl_____p	h__m

Challenge your students to make as many real words as possible by filling in appropriate vowels.

- Use the "every student response" technique by issuing two cards to each student—one marked "yes" and the other marked "no." Have your students use the cards to answer questions in short oral exercises. For example, ask:

Does dog *have a long /o/ sound?* (no)

Does beat *have a long /e/ sound?* (yes)

Have your students respond simultaneously by holding up the card of their choice.

Teaching Vocabulary in Context

Factors to Consider When Interpreting Student Performance

The use of context is as important a word recognition skill at the beginning stages of reading instruction as it is for more advanced readers.

Tips for Teaching Vocabulary in Context

Have your students ask themselves such questions as *Does this word make sense in this sentence? Does this word fit the meaning of the story?* To help your students practice using context when reading, try these activities:

■ Develop cloze exercises by deleting words from paragraphs or short stories and replacing them with blanks. Ask your students to read the selection and try to replace the missing word with one that is meaningful. Extend the lesson by asking your students to circle the parts of the sentence that provided clues to the correct word choice. The use of this modification will show you whether your students are focusing on meaningful context clues.

■ Have each student choose five words from a social studies or science lesson and write a sentence for each word, leaving a blank where the word should go. Invite your students to read the sentences aloud to classmates who try to guess the target word by using the context clues. This activity can help students become sensitive to how authors use context clues to aid readers in understanding what they write.

■ On heavy paper, write sentences that are rich in context, then cut each sentence apart into its word parts. Distribute each sentence to a group of students, one word to each student. Have the group work together to reassemble the sentence into a meaningful order.

■ In a group situation, when you encounter a new, unknown word in context, ask students questions such as the following:
  — *What do you think the word means? What clues do you have?*
  — (Use the word in a sentence that broadens the meaning of the word.) *Now what do you think the word means?*
  — (Use the word in a sentence that narrows the meaning of the word.) *Now what do you think the word means?*

Continue with examples and questions about the word until students have a good understanding of the word's meaning.

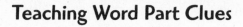

Teaching Word Part Clues

Factors to Consider When Interpreting Student Performance

Consider your students' *Instructional Reading Level* to determine what type of instructional program is most appropriate. Generally, the *Instructional Reading Levels* for grades 2 through 5 require a high degree of emphasis on teaching word part clues. Your students should have learned sound-letter matching before you teach them the use of word part clues. Skill in using word part clues depends upon your students' ability to use phonic skills to decode the root word.

Tips for Teaching Word Part Clues

- The end result of instruction in the use of word part clues should be the ability to derive meaning from context. Whenever possible, let this instruction grow out of your students' discovery of unknown words they encounter in context. When your students have learned how to use word part clues within a context, they will be able to determine the meaning of a sentence or even the author's intent by the use of a particular clue.

- Teach the analysis of word part clues using root words that your students recognize.

- Teach word part clues using prefixes, suffixes, inflectional endings, and compound words that are new and interesting and that students will relate to and remember.

- Teach the use of word part clues along with vocabulary in context.

- Avoid interrupting a student who is in the midst of an enjoyable reading experience. If a student has difficulty recognizing a word, and if other more rapid or already acquired skills do not unlock the word, simply supply it. Note the word as an opportunity for a later lesson that focuses on the use of word part clues.

Here are some exercises that help students learn to use words in context:

- Have your students complete sentences by inserting the correct form of the missing adjective or adverb. For example:

James is the _____ runner on our team.

fast

At first, supply students with choices of endings. After guided practice, eliminate the choices so that students develop their own meaningful responses.

- Give your students a list of words that have suffixes (e.g., *running, slower, telling, smoothest*). Ask them to write or say aloud to the group two sentences for each word—one for the root word and one for the root word with the suffix. Try this same activity with prefixes.

- Provide your students with a list of root words and suffixes. Have them match the root words to as many of the suffixes as possible and write a sentence for each match.

- Divide the class into two teams. Write a prefix on the board (e.g. *pre, dis, re*). Have a player from Team A go to the board and write a word containing the given prefix. Then a player from Team B should write a sentence that correctly uses the other team's word in meaningful context. Continue through the teams until all students have had an opportunity to play.

Teaching Fluency

Factors to Consider When Interpreting Student Performance

Your students' performance on the Fluency Test should be interpreted in light of what you already know about the students from working with them in various classroom activities, as well as in light of their performance on other tests within *Rigby READS*. You may find that a student performs much better on the test than you might expect from the oral reading ability that he or she has demonstrated in your classroom. This may indicate that this student needs to be encouraged to read aloud more in class and independently. On the other hand, you may find that some students who appear to be fairly fluent readers may actually experience difficulty on the Fluency Test. You should also be cautious about students who do not do well on the test because the one-on-one situation can be intimidating to some students. Shyness or anxiety may cause a student to underperform on the Fluency Test.

If a student does not exhibit fluent reading on the Fluency Test, it is essential to determine whether the problem lies with the student's phonemic awareness or decoding abilities. An examination of the student's performance on the objectives assessed on *Rigby READS* should reveal his or her strengths and weaknesses in the fundamental skill areas that impact the ability to read fluently and comprehend texts.

Following are guidelines for evaluating a student's performance on the Fluency Test. Scores are determined by words read correctly per minute (WCPM). Target scores reflect goals for a student taking the Fluency Test at his or her *Instructional Reading Level*.

By readministering the Fluency Test at the end of the school year, you can measure how much a student's Reading Fluency has progressed. Another way to interpret a student's Reading Fluency is to compare the student's performance to how other students have scored on reading fluency. The table on the next page provides norms based on information gained from the administration of fluency tests to 7,000 to 9,000 students in five western and midwestern states.

The scores in the table are Words Correct Per Minute (WCPM), which is determined by subtracting the number of incorrect words from the number of words read in one minute.

The table is used to determine a student's ranking in comparison to the norm group. For example, if a student was administered the Fluency Assessment in the middle of the year and the student's WCPM was 95, he would be in the group whose percentile ranking was from the 26th to the 50th percentile. The four percentile rankings can be interpreted as being much below, slightly below, slightly above, and much above the average of the norm group.

Grade 5 Fluency Norm Table

| Time of Year Tested | | | Norm Comparison | |
| Beginning | Middle | End | | |
WCPM	WCPM	WCPM	Percentile Group	Comparison to the Norm Group
77 and below	93 and below	100 and below	1 to 25	Much Below
78 to 105	94 to 118	101 to 128	26 to 50	Slightly Below
106 to 126	119 to 143	129 to 151	51 to 75	Slightly Above
127 and above	144 and above	151 and above	76 to 99	Much Above

Tips for Teaching Fluency

To help your students develop as fluent readers, provide opportunities for practice with a wide variety of appealing activities so that they are not merely trying to read rapidly. Some suggestions for learning activities that promote fluency include:

■ Model fluent reading by reading aloud to students and discussing the characteristics of fluent reading. Expose your students to a wide variety of genres, including poetry, speeches, and folk and fairy tales with rich, lyrical language. Incorporate professional recordings of texts being read aloud.

■ Provide opportunities for independent practice in texts that reflect your students' *Instructional Reading Levels*. Research shows that readers need to read texts at their *Instructional Reading Level* to improve fluency. Have your students read aloud a text of their choice for one minute. Do this each week and have each student keep a graph of his or her reading speed. Be sure to encourage your students to read for both meaning and accuracy.

- Provide regular opportunities for your students to read aloud in pairs or in small groups. Develop a checklist that states the characteristics of fluent reading. Have one reader read a selection aloud and have another assess whether the reader is reading smoothly and fluently. The checklist should include such things as:
  - read so that the story was interesting
  - showed expression by changing tone
  - read smoothly
  - read words correctly

- Make reading aloud a part of regular classroom instruction, while keeping in mind your students' comfort level. Some activities include choral readings and group oral reports and presentations.

- Use a Readers' Theatre approach to teaching text. Have students read dialogue or other segments of a text suited for performance before an audience.

- Encourage parents to help students practice fluent reading at home.

Chapter 5
Test Development

How the Tests Were Developed

The content of the *Rigby READS* assessment series is based on the sixth edition of the *Metropolitan Achievement Tests* (MAT). The MAT has been one of the most respected and widely used achievement tests chosen by the nation's schools since 1930.

The Foundation of *Rigby READS*

Rigby READS focuses on three perceived needs of educators in today's schools.

■ First, there is a need on the part of classroom teachers for accurate but quick assessment of each student's current level of reading comprehension, preferably on a group basis. This information is critical to assigning reading tasks that are on the correct level—i.e., challenging, but not so difficult as to be frustrating or to require constant teacher intervention.

■ Second, there is a need for diagnostic information, especially for students whose current level of achievement is low.

■ Finally, administrators seek the results of the above sets of information in an easily summarized and interpretable form that could result in effective leadership of a sound reading program.

These requests for reading levels, diagnostic information, and instructionally useful summaries in an efficient and technically superior form led to the development of *Rigby READS*, which consists of a series of *Diagnostic Tests* that assess a student's achievement in each of the major skill areas of reading.

Many instruments provide a reading diagnosis for students; however, almost all such instruments are individually administered, thus requiring both a trained administrator and a large amount of time to collect information for large groups. *Rigby READS* provides this information concurrently for *groups* of students. Thus all of the *READS* tests (with the exception of the Phonemic Awareness Test and an optional Fluency Test) are group-administered. Teachers can focus on the *accuracy* of test scores and the *importance* and *representativeness* of test content, or its *reliability* and *validity*.

Content and Structure of *Rigby READS*

All reading selections and test items on *Rigby READS*, including corresponding artwork, were reviewed by highly experienced reading professionals for such issues as appropriateness, timeliness, and potential bias. Approximately 93% of the test items included in *Rigby READS* were drawn from the *Metropolitan Achievement Tests, Sixth Edition* (MAT6). This is a critical aspect of the technical superiority of the *READS* product, as the MAT6 series was developed over a period of six years. Its development involved more than three years of content development by trained, experienced reading and assessment professionals.

Test Item Construction and Tryout

As part of the development of the MAT6 series, all test items were field tested nationally using a sample of approximately 22,000 students. Schools included in this research activity were selected to represent the national school population in terms of geographic region, school system enrollment, and socioeconomic status. The item analysis field-test research program provided data on the empirical difficulty level of each item (both traditional p-value and Rasch item difficulties), the percent of students choosing each option as the answer to the item, and the relationship between item response and total score on the test (point-biserial discrimination indices). Data in this program were collected for the grade at which the test item was ultimately intended, as well as for one grade above and one grade below. This design permitted the movement of items to adjacent grades if student performance indicated a more appropriate fit to a grade other than that originally intended. It also permitted an inspection of all test items for their appropriateness for assessing growth over time.

National Standardization Research

The MAT6 Diagnostic tests were standardized nationally using a sample of approximately 70,000 students in grades K through 8; the Reading Comprehension tests were also standardized using a separate sample of more than 300,000 students. Schools participating in the national standardization program were selected to represent the nation's school population with respect to geographic region, school system enrollment, public vs. private affiliation, and, most critically, socioeconomic status.

Because the *Instructional Reading Level* scores are so integral to the *Rigby READS* series and its interpretation, several validation studies were conducted to confirm the accuracy of these scores. The results are summarized on the next two pages.

1. Teachers judged the grade level of each MAT reading passage during the national standardization program. No indications were available to them of the designated levels of the passages. Teacher ratings closely followed the assigned grade levels both within and across test levels.

2. When *Instructional Reading Levels* assigned to students on the basis of their MAT scores were studied relative to other reading level estimates (tests in the students' basal reader, cloze tests, or informal reading inventories), the estimates of *Instructional Reading Levels* were all highly intercorrelated. MAT-based *Instructional Reading Levels* estimates had a higher correlation with each of the other methods than did any of the other methods with one another. This information is presented more fully in an article by Smith and Beck, which is referenced at the end of this manual.

3. Extensive analysis of both the standardization data and the final versions of *Rigby READS* indicates anticipated relationships between grade levels of reading passages and the difficulty of questions based on these passages. The higher the level of the passage, the lower the student performance. This is a critical element of the validation of the *Rigby READS Instructional Reading Levels*. It is possible to write very difficult test items for rather easy reading selections and vice versa. However, in order for *Rigby READS* to provide valid estimates of *Instructional Reading Levels*, the difficulty of test items must match the difficulty of the passages.

Test Reliability

The reliability of any test is one indication of the confidence that may be placed in the scores resulting from the test. The test data presented for *Rigby READS* are Kuder-Richardson reliability estimates, which provide a measure of the instrument's internal consistency.

Reliability coefficients (r_{tt}) and standard errors of measurement (SE_M) are presented in the table on the facing page. The standard error of measurement is a statistical estimate of how closely a student's obtained raw score is to his or her theoretical true score. It indicates the range of raw scores within which a student, if tested multiple times using parallel forms of the same test, would likely score. Kuder-Richardson reliability coefficients presented in the table are based on the on-level sample of students in the MAT6 standardization, adjusted as appropriate because of changes in the test content of *Rigby READS*. Reliability data are presented both for the Reading Comprehension Test and for all components of the *Diagnostic Test*.

Kuder-Richardson 20 Internal-Consistency Reliability Estimates and Raw Score Standard Errors of Measurement for End of Grade 5

Test Name	Number of Items	Form A		Form B	
		KR 20	SE$_m$	KR 20	SE$_m$
Sounds-Letters: Consonants	24	.86	1.7	.83	1.7
Sounds-Letters: Vowels	42	.94	2.3	.90	2.5
Vocabulary in Context	24	.85	1.7	.83	1.9
Word Part Clues	18	.82	1.6	.79	1.7
Reading Comprehension	48	.89	2.8	.89	2.8

Test Validity

A test is content valid if the underlying measured objectives and test items adequately cover the curricular areas the test is intended to measure. Since each school district's curriculum differs, each potential user must determine the content validity of *Rigby READS*. To assist schools in judging the content validity of *Rigby READS*, a Compendium of Objectives Across All Test Levels listing all objectives measured by the tests is presented on pages 88–91 in the Appendix.

The content coverage of *Rigby READS* was validated at four stages in its development.

- First, the authors based the test blueprints on an extensive analysis of textbooks and other curricular materials in wide use nationally. Special attention during this phase was paid to the report and recommendations of the National Reading Panel.

- Second, content editors, all former teachers holding advanced degrees in education or an English-language area, verified the selection and grade placement of the proposed objectives to be assessed.

- Third, curriculum experts from around the nation confirmed the match of the objectives to current school syllabi. Thousands of students throughout the nation demonstrated the appropriateness of the items and objectives by their performances on the tests during the various large-scale research programs.

- Finally, teachers participating in the standardization programs affirmed that these were the instructional objectives currently being taught at the tested grade level.

Comparability between Paper-and-Pencil and Computer-Based Tests

Computers have become an integral part of education, shaping every aspect of instruction, including the delivery of a wide variety of assessments. Although there are many benefits associated with delivering tests on a computer, there is the potential that the mode of delivery might change the constructs that the test was designed to measure, and therefore result in statistically significant score differences.

The methods employed to determine equivalence between paper-and-pencil test administration and computer-based testing have consisted primarily of correlational studies comparing mean total scores or individual item scores (or both) obtained by examinees on parallel paper-and-pencil and computerized versions of the same test. Exclusive of studies involving computer-adaptive testing, a number of narrative reviews have been done on the topic of comparability between paper-and-pencil testing and computer-based testing (Bugbee, 1996; Mazzeo & Harvey, 1988; Mead & Drasgow, 1993; Wise & Plake, 1989), as have individual studies (Boo & Vispoel, 1998; Evans, Tannehill, & Martin, 1995; Kobrin & Young, 2003). For the most part, these studies have reported that the comparability of scores using these two test modes are inconclusive.

The best way to ensure consistent interpretation of scores between these test modalities is to conduct comparability studies to examine the magnitude of these effects. Alternatively when comparability studies do not exist, every effort should be made to ensure the mode of test delivery is consistent for a given cohort of examinees as an aid to coherent score interpretation. Additionally when choosing computer-delivered assessments, it is important that students take exams on computers with which they are already familiar and that testing cohorts use equipment that provides consistent screen size, quality screen resolution and refresh rates, as well as sufficient processor and Internet connection speeds to reduce any technology-related effects on student performance.

A final consideration regarding interpretation issues between paper-and-pencil and computer-based test scores is related to whether the test in question is considered a high-stakes or low-stakes assessment. Because most classroom-based assessment is of a low-stakes variety, any potential comparability issues must be tempered with existing knowledge about a given student's abilities. This information allows teachers to make professional judgments about student mastery that will permit the creation of a rich prescriptive pathway which will best advance learning for each student.

Appendix

Directions for Administering the Fluency Test

The *Rigby READS* Fluency Test is an individually administered oral reading test that helps you evaluate each student's speed, accuracy, phrasing, syntax, and expression.

Prior to testing:

- Read the test directions and the scoring directions carefully before administering the test.

- Provide the student with a copy of the fluency test. Allow the student an opportunity to practice reading the passage aloud several times prior to testing.

- Make another copy of the test that will serve as a place for you to make notes for scoring. This copy can also serve as a record of the student's performance.

- Plan to test the student in a quiet area away from other students and class activity. You will need to give each student one minute for reading, plus you will need time at the beginning of the reading to get the student started and at the end to calculate scores. A single student assessment should take about five to seven minutes.

- You may want to use a timer during testing so that you need not watch a clock in addition to taking notes about the student's reading.

During testing:

- Put the student at ease. Tell him or her that reading aloud is an important part of reading, and that you will be listening and taking notes as he or she reads a story for one minute.

- If you think the student may finish reading the passage before the minute is up, tell him or her to then start over from the beginning. Note that most students will not finish the entire passage before the minute is up.

- Have the student read the passage out loud as you time him or her. Record the number of word call errors the student makes while reading. Word call errors include mispronouncing, omitting, repeating, or transposing words. Mark in the text where the student leaves off at the end of one minute.

After testing:

■ Calculate the student's numerical score for speed and accuracy. That score is derived by subtracting the number of errors from the number of words read per minute.

■ Assign a ranking based on your overall observations of the students':
   — **phrasing**: intonation, stress, and pausing;
   — **syntax**: adherence to the order of words;
   — **expression**: ability to convey feeling, anticipation, or characterization according to this scale:

Level 4: Reads primarily in larger, meaningful phrase groups.
Consistently preserves author's syntax.
Most of the story is read with expressive interpretation.
Some regressions, repetitions, or deviation from the text may occur, but they do not detract from the overall meaning of the passage.

Level 3: Reads primarily three- to four-word phrase groups, with some smaller groups present.
The majority of the phrasing is appropriate and the syntax is preserved.
Little or no expressive interpretation is present, but the reading generally sounds meaningful.

Level 2: Reads primarily two-word phrase groups, with some larger groups as well as some word-by-word reading.
Word groupings may seem awkward or unrelated to the larger context of sentence or passage.
The reading sounds as if the reader does not understand what the text is about.
There is little or no expression.

Level 1: Reads primarily word-by-word.
Occasional two- or three-word phrases may occur, but these are infrequent and/or they do not preserve a meaningful syntax.
The reader does not understand what the text is about.
There is no expression.

■ If you choose to administer the Fluency Test a second time, compare the student's rankings for the two tests to measure his or her progress.

8	A shrewd farmer and her neighbor had been
18	longtime rivals. But because they lived next door to one
27	another, they sometimes helped each other. It should be
37	said that they really only pretended to help each other,
49	just in case one really did need the other's help one day.
57	One spring the foes planted carrots together, agreeing
70	to divide the crop. The neighbor had a plan to get it all
79	at harvest. Believing all crops grow above ground, he
89	persuaded the farmer to give him the green tops. The
98	farmer happily went along. Then she took the carrots
106	from the ground. Next they planted cucumbers. Learning
116	from the carrot incident, the neighbor decided to ask for
125	everything under the ground. The farmer smiled as she
133	picked the cucumbers growing above the ground and
142	left her outraged neighbor the roots. Determined to get
152	even, the neighbor agreed to raise corn with the farmer
162	if he could have both what grew above and below
172	ground. But at harvest time, the farmer removed the ears
183	and left the neighbor the stalks and roots. That was the
188	neighbor's last attempt at farming.

Student's Name: _____ Date: _____

Speed/Accuracy: WCPM score calculation

Total Words Read Per Minute	Total Number of Errors	Words Correct Per Minute (WCPM)

Observations: Level Rank (circle one)

Level 4
Level 3
Level 2
Level 1

Grade 5, Form A *Evaluation Test* Answer Key

1. D	25. A
2. G	26. H
3. C	27. A
4. F	28. G
5. D	29. B
6. E	30. H
7. A	31. B
8. G	32. G
9. C	33. B
10. F	34. A
11. B	35. C
12. F	36. H
13. C	37. D
14. F	38. G
15. D	39. C
16. F	40. E
17. D	41. B
18. G	42. F
19. A	43. A
20. F	44. F
21. B	45. C
22. E	46. H
23. C	47. C
24. F	48. F

Grade 5, Form A *Diagnostic Test* Answer Key

Sounds-Letters: Consonants

1. A	5. C	9. D	13. C	17. B	21. C
2. E	6. G	10. F	14. F	18. F	22. H
3. B	7. D	11. C	15. D	19. D	23. C
4. E	8. F	12. E	16. F	20. E	24. F

Sounds-Letters: Vowels

1. B	8. F	15. C	22. F	29. D	36. G
2. G	9. C	16. F	23. D	30. G	37. D
3. C	10. F	17. C	24. E	31. B	38. G
4. H	11. A	18. E	25. B	32. E	39. B
5. C	12. E	19. C	26. G	33. A	40. F
6. H	13. D	20. E	27. D	34. G	41. C
7. C	14. F	21. B	28. F	35. D	42. H

Vocabulary in Context

1. C	5. B	9. B	13. B	17. D	21. C
2. H	6. F	10. F	14. G	18. E	22. G
3. A	7. D	11. A	15. B	19. D	23. B
4. E	8. E	12. G	16. G	20. H	24. G

Word Part Clues

1. B	4. F	7. D	10. H	13. A	16. E
2. G	5. A	8. H	11. C	14. F	17. B
3. D	6. G	9. C	12. F	15. C	18. H

Reading Comprehension

1. D	9. C	17. D	25. A	33. B	41. B
2. G	10. F	18. G	26. H	34. A	42. F
3. C	11. B	19. A	27. A	35. C	43. A
4. F	12. F	20. F	28. G	36. H	44. F
5. D	13. C	21. B	29. B	37. D	45. C
6. E	14. F	22. E	30. H	38. G	46. H
7. A	15. D	23. C	31. B	39. C	47. C
8. G	16. F	24. F	32. G	40. E	48. F

1. B	25. D
2. E	26. F
3. C	27. C
4. H	28. G
5. C	29. A
6. F	30. F
7. C	31. A
8. E	32. F
9. D	33. D
10. E	34. E
11. B	35. B
12. H	36. G
13. A	37. A
14. G	38. E
15. A	39. D
16. G	40. F
17. B	41. C
18. H	42. H
19. C	43. A
20. F	44. C
21. C	45. F
22. E	46. A
23. A	47. F
24. E	48. D

Grade 5, Form B *Diagnostic Test* Answer Key

Sounds-Letters: Consonants

1. B	5. D	9. D	13. B	17. A	21. C
2. F	6. E	10. F	14. G	18. F	22. F
3. A	7. B	11. C	15. D	19. A	23. C
4. G	8. H	12. E	16. E	20. G	24. G

Sounds-Letters: Vowels

1. D	8. G	15. C	22. H	29. D	36. E
2. F	9. B	16. H	23. A	30. G	37. B
3. D	10. H	17. C	24. H	31. A	38. G
4. F	11. C	18. E	25. A	32. E	39. B
5. A	12. H	19. C	26. G	33. D	40. F
6. E	13. C	20. E	27. A	34. F	41. C
7. B	14. F	21. B	28. G	35. A	42. H

Vocabulary in Context

1. B	5. A	9. C	13. B	17. B	21. A
2. G	6. E	10. F	14. G	18. E	22. G
3. B	7. D	11. A	15. B	19. C	23. D
4. F	8. E	12. F	16. H	20. H	24. E

Word Part Clues

1. A	4. H	7. D	10. H	13. A	16. E
2. G	5. A	8. E	11. C	14. F	17. B
3. D	6. G	9. C	12. F	15. C	18. D

Reading Comprehension

1. B	9. D	17. B	25. D	33. D	41. C
2. E	10. E	18. H	26. F	34. E	42. H
3. C	11. B	19. C	27. C	35. B	43. A
4. H	12. H	20. F	28. G	36. G	44. G
5. C	13. A	21. C	29. A	37. A	45. B
6. F	14. G	22. E	30. F	38. E	46. E
7. C	15. A	23. A	31. A	39. D	47. B
8. E	16. G	24. E	32. F	40. F	48. H

Student *Evaluation Test* Report Blackline Master

Name _____ Grade _____

Teacher _____ Date Tested _____

Test Administered: Grade _____ Form _____

Functional Reading Levels

Instructional Reading Level	*Independent Reading Level*

Reading Skills Order of Importance

High Importance	
Some Importance	
Low Importance	

Reading Comprehension Skills and Strategies

Reading Skills and Strategies	*Criterion Score*
Literal Comprehension	
Inferential Comprehension	
Critical Comprehension	

Action Plan

For Recommended Reading List:
WEB www.harcourtachieve.com/READS • **PHONE** 1-800-531-5015 • **FAX** 1-800-699-9458

Class *Evaluation Test* Report Blackline Master

Name _____ Grade _____

Teacher _____ Date Tested _____

Test Administered: Grade _____ Form _____

Evaluation Test Results Summary

Reading Level	Below Grade Level	On Grade Level	Above Grade Level
Number of Students			

Reading Level	2-4 minus	3-1 to 3-2	3-3	4-1 to 4-3	5-1 to 5-3	6-1 to 6-2	7 plus
Instructional Number of Students							
Percent of Class							
Independent Number of Students							
Percent of Class							

Student	Instructional Reading Level	Independent Reading Level

RIGBY READS
Reading Evaluation and
Diagnostic System

Name _____ Grade _____

Teacher _____ Date Tested _____

Test Administered: Grade _____ Form _____

Functional Reading Levels

Instructional Reading Level	Independent Reading Level

Reading Skills in Order of Importance

Importance	Reading Skill/Strategy	Criterion Score
High		
Some		
Low		

Criterion Scores

	Number Possible	Number Correct	Criterion Score
Sounds-Letters: Consonants Total			
Beginning Consonants			
Ending Consonants			
Sounds-Letters: Vowels Total			
Short Vowels			
Long Vowels			
Digraphs/ Diphthongs			

	Number Possible	Number Correct	Criterion Score
Word Part Clues Total			
Inflections/ Prefixes			
Vocabulary in Context Total			
Reading Comprehension Total			
Literal			
Inferential			
Critical			

For Recommended Reading List:
WEB www.harcourtachieve.com/READS • **PHONE** 1-800-531-5015 • **FAX** 1-800-699-9458

Name _____ Grade _____

Teacher _____ Date Tested _____

Test Administered: Grade _____ Form _____

Diagnostic Test Results Summary

Reading Level	Below Grade Level	On Grade Level	Above Grade Level
Number of Students			

Reading Level or Reading Skill	2-4 minus	3-1 to 3-2	3-3	4-1 to 4-3	5-1 to 5-3	6-1 to 6-2	7 plus
Instructional Level Number of Students							
Percent of Class							
Independent Level Number of Students							
Percent of Class							

	Proficient	Developing	Beginning
Sounds-Letters: Consonants Number of Students			
Percent of Class			
Sounds-Letters: Vowels Number of Students			
Percent of Class			
Word Part Clues Number of Students			
Percent of Class			
Vocabulary Number of Students			
Percent of Class			
Comprehension Number of Students			
Percent of Class			

Student Names	Functional Reading Levels		Performance on Reading Skills and Strategies						
	Instructional Reading Level	Independent Reading Level	Sounds-Letters: Consonants	Sounds-Letters: Vowels	Word Part Clues	Vocabulary	Comprehension		
							Literal	Inferential	Critical

Student Yearly Progress Report

Student _____   Grade _____

School _____   Date _____

Teacher _____

READS Reading Comprehension Progress

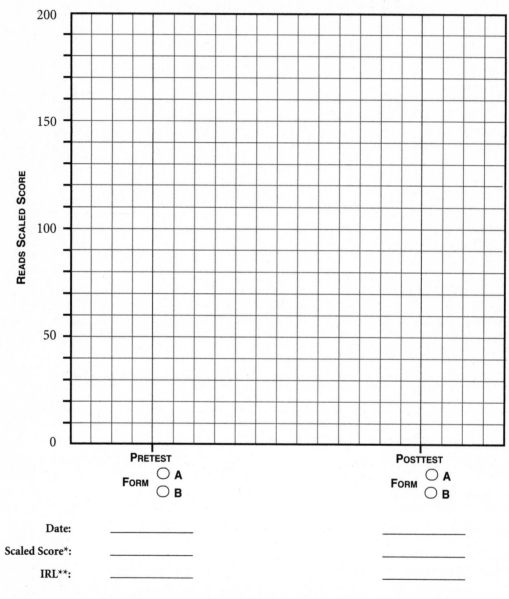

	PRETEST	POSTTEST
Date:	_____	_____
Scaled Score*:	_____	_____
IRL**:	_____	_____

Scaled Score—These scores express the results of READS Reading Comprehension for both Forms A and B of either the *Evaluation Test* or the Reading Comprehension sitting of the *Diagnostic Test* and all grade levels (1–8) on a single common scale. These scores are useful in measuring change in reading achievement over a period of time. See pages 99 to 100 for information on Scaled Scores.

**IRL*—This is the student's *Instructional Reading Level.*

Class Yearly Progress Report

RIGBY READS
Reading Evaluation and
Diagnostic System

School _____   Grade _____

Teacher _____   School Year _____

READS Reading Comprehension Progress by Student

	Student	READS Test Dates		READS Scaled Scores*			
		Pre	Post	Pre	Post	Gain	SS Growth
Above-Level Readers							
On-Level Readers							
Below-Level Readers							
	Class Average						

Scaled Score—These scores express the results of READS Reading Comprehension for both Forms A and B of either the *Evaluation Test* or the Reading Comprehension sitting of the *Diagnostic Test* and all grade levels (1–8) on a single common scale. These scores are useful in measuring change in reading achievement over a period of time. See pages 99 to 100 for information on Scaled Scores. A student with negative growth in reading achievement will not have a bar graph in the right column.

Student: _____

Grade: _____

Date: _____

Dear Parent or Caregiver:

Your child has completed the *Rigby Reading Evaluation and Diagnostic System (Rigby READS)* test. This test is designed to measure your child's ability in the reading skills most needed to obtain comprehension at your child's level of reading development.

Test Date	
Independent Reading Level	
Instructional Reading Level	

At the *Independent Reading Level*, your child can read with high accuracy and comprehension. Your child will need some help with reading at his or her *Instructional Reading Level*. Selecting books at the appropriate level encourages your child to read more, which is critical to academic success.

There are a variety of things you can do to enhance your child's reading progress. Here are some suggestions. Choose the ones that work best for you.

■ Your child's teacher can suggest books that your child can read independently. However, children at this age often like to share what they have read. Ask your child to read you a favorite part of a story. Talking about what happens in a story will help your child understand and remember what he or she has read.

■ Your child can become a better reader by learning to use reading for all kinds of activities. Reading about a place you are going to visit, reading recipes, or reading computer guides will help your child learn how useful reading is. Word games in which your child categorizes words by their meaning or by how they relate to certain activities will help improve your child's vocabulary.

■ Help your child find books that are of interest at his or her *Independent Reading Level*. Ask you child's teacher or the school librarian for suggestions for book titles. Tell them what your child does for fun, and they will be able to provide you with titles of books on those topics.

Here are some books for this student's *Independent Reading Level*.

If you have any questions about your child's score, please contact me.

Sincerely,

Estudiante:_____

Grado:_____

Fecha:_____

Estimado padre o tutor:

Su hijo ha tomado el sistema de evaluación y diagnóstico de lectura *Rigby Reading Evaluation and Diagnostic System (Rigby READS)*. Esta prueba está diseñada para medir la habilidad que tiene su hijo en las destrezas importantes de la lectura.

Fecha de la Prueba	
Nivel de Lectura Independiente	
Nivel de Lectura Educacional	

En el *Nivel de Lectura Independente*, su hijo puede leer perfectamente y comprende lo que lee. Su hijo necesita ayuda adicional para leer a su *Nivel de Lectura Educacional*. Es importante seleccionar libros apropiados a su nivel, para animar a su hijo a leer más, lo cual es indispensable para lograr éxito académico.

Usted puede hacer varias cosas para ayudar a su hijo a progresar en lectura. A continuación se dan unas sugerencias. Escoja las que funcionen mejor para usted.

- El maestro de su hijo le puede sugerir algunos libros que su hijo pueda leer solo. Sin embargo, los niños a esta edad, con frecuencia les gusta compartir lo que han leído. Pídale a su hijo que le lea la parte que más le guste de una historia. Hablen acerca de lo que pasa en la historia, esto le ayudará a su hijo a entender y recordar lo que ha leído.

- Su hijo puede convertirse en un mejor lector si aprende a usar la lectura en todo tipo de actividades. Le ayudará a entender lo útil que es la lectura si lee acerca de un lugar que van a ir a visita, las recetas de cocina o unas manuales para la computadora. Los juegos de palabras en los que su hijo pone las palabras en diferentes categorías según su significado o en los que agrupa las palabras relacionadas con ciertas actividades, le ayudarán a enriquecer su vocabulario.

- Ayude a su hijo a encontrar libros que sean interesantes de acuerdo a su *Nivel de Lectura Independiente*. Pídale al maestro de su hijo o al bibliotecario de su escuela que le sugiera algunos títulos de libros. Dígales cuales son los pasatiempos favoritos de su hijo, para que ellos puedan sugerirle libros de acuerdo a los intereses de su hijo.

A continuación hay una lista de libros en el *Nivel de Lectura Independiente* de su hijo.

Si usted tiene alguna pregunta relacionada con la calificación de su hijo, por favor comuníquese conmigo.

Atentamente,

Instructional and Independent Reading Level Cut Scores for the Grade 5 Test

Test Materials Level	Items	Instructional Reading Level	Cut Score	Independent Reading Level
Grade 3	5	2-4 minus	0–7	1-7 minus
		3-1	8–11	2-1
		3-2	12–14	2-2
		3-3	15–17	2-3
Grade 4	11	4-1	18–21	3-1
		4-2	22–25	3-2
		4-3	26–29	3-3
Grade 5	16	5-1	30–32	4-1
		5-2	33–35	4-2
		5-3	36–38	4-3
Grade 6	11	6-1	39–42	5-1
		6-2	43–45	5-2
Grade 7/8	5	7 plus	45–48	6-1 plus
Total	48			

The Importance of Reading Skills for Grade 5 as Determined by *Instructional Reading Levels*

Instructional Reading Levels

Reading Skills Tests	Kinder-garten	1-1 to 1-2	1-3 to 1-4	1-5 to 1-7	2-1 to 2-2	2-3 to 2-4	3-1 to 3-3	4-1 to 4-3	5-1 to 5-3	6-1 to 6-2	7 to 8	9 to 10
Visual Discrimination	High	Some	Some	Low	Low	Low	—	—	—	—	—	—
Letter Recognition	Low	High	High	Some	Some	Low	—	—	—	—	—	—
Auditory Discrimination	High	High	High	Some	Low	Low	—	—	—	—	—	—
Sounds-Letters: Consonants	Low	Some	High	High	High	Some	Some	Low	Low	—	—	—
Sounds-Letters: Vowels	—	—	—	Some	High	High	High	Some	Some	Some	Low	Low
Vocabulary in Context	High	High	High	High	High	High	High	High	High	High	High	High
Word Part Clues	—	Low	Low	Some	Some	Some	High	High	High	High	Some	Some
Skimming and Scanning	—	—	—	—	Low	Low	Low	Some	Some	High	High	High

Cut Score Criteria for the Grade 5 Test

Test	Objectives	Number Possible	Beginning	Developing	Proficient
			Criterion Score Levels		
Sounds-Letters: Consonants		24	0–13	14–18	19–24
	Initial Consonants: Single, Clusters, Digraphs	9	0–5	6–7	8–9
	Final Consonants: Single, Clusters, Digraphs	9	0–5	6–7	8–9
	Silent Letters	6	0–2	3–4	5–6
Sounds-Letters: Vowels		42	0–19	20–31	32–42
	Short Vowels: a, e, i, o, u	15	0–7	8–11	12–15
	Long Vowels: a, e, i, o, u	15	0–7	8–11	12–15
	Digraphs and Diphthongs	12	0–5	6–9	10–12
Vocabulary in Context		24	0–9	10–20	21–24
Word Part Clues	Affixes (Prefixes, Suffixes, and Inflections)	18	0–9	10–14	15–18
Reading Comprehension		48			
	Literal Comprehension	15	0–6	7–13	14–15
	Inferential Comprehension	19	0–8	9–16	17–19
	Critical Comprehension	14	0–6	7–11	12–14

Action Plans for the Grade 5 Test
Instructional Reading Levels

2-4 minus

- This fifth-grade student is reading much below grade placement. It is recommended that the student be administered the Grade 4 level of *Rigby READS*.

- The best estimate of the instructional level of books you should use with this student is 2-4 or below. The student will need some help with books at this level.

- The reading comprehension skills and their importance for this student are listed above on this report. He or she should be able to read independently books at a 1-7 level.

- The reading skills and strategies this student needs help with to make progress as a reader are Sounds-Letters: Vowels, and Vocabulary in Context. The student might need some help with Sounds-Letters: Consonants.

- If the student does well with these areas, you should work next on Word Part Clues.

- If the student struggles with these skills, you may want to administer the Phonemic Awareness Test, which is included in the Teacher's Manual for the Beginning Reader, Grade 1, and Grade 2 Tests.

3-1 to 3-3

- The best estimate of the instructional level of books you should use with this student is 3-1 to 3-3. The student will need some help with books at this level.

- The reading comprehension skills and their importance for this student are listed above on this report. He or she should be able to read independently books at a 2-1 level.

- The reading skills and strategies this student needs help with to make further progress as a reader are Vocabulary in Context and Sounds-Letters: Vowels. It may also be helpful to spend some time on Sounds-Letters: Consonants.

- If the student becomes proficient in these areas, the next area of attention should be Word Part Clues.

4-1 to 4-3

- The best estimate of the instructional level of books you should use with this student is 4-1 to 4-3. The student will need some help with books at this level.

- The reading comprehension skills and their importance for this student are listed above on this report. He or she should be able to read independently books at a 3-1 level.

- The reading skills and strategies this student needs help with to make further progress as a reader are Vocabulary in Context and Word Part Clues. It might also be helpful to spend some time on Sounds-Letters: Vowels.

5-1 to 5-3

- The best estimate of the instructional level of books you should use with this student is 5-1 to 5-3. The student will need some help with books at this level.

- The reading comprehension skills and their importance for this student are listed above on this report. He or she should be able to read independently books at a 4-1 level.

- The reading skills and strategies this student needs help with to make further progress as a reader are Vocabulary in Context and Word Part Clues. You might also find that this student needs some help with Sounds-Letters: Vowels.

- This student is ready for instruction in Skimming and Scanning. The Skimming and Scanning Test can be found in the grade 6 materials.

6-1 to 6-2

- The best estimate of the instructional level of books you should use with this student is 6-1 to 6-2. The student will need some help with books at this level.

- The reading comprehension skills and their importance for this student are listed above on this report. He or she should be able to read independently books at a 5-1 level.

- The reading skills and strategies this student needs help with to make further progress as a reader are Vocabulary in Context, Word Part Clues, and Skimming and Scanning. The Skimming and Scanning Test can be found in the grade 6 materials.

7 plus

- This fifth-grade student is reading two or more years above grade placement. It is recommended that the student be administered the Grade 6 Level of *Rigby READS*.

- The best estimate of the instructional level of books you should use with this student is 7. The student may need some help with books at this level.

- The reading comprehension skills and their importance for this student are listed above on this report. He or she should be able to read independently books at a 6-1 or above level.

- The reading skills and strategies this student needs help with to make further progress as a reader are Vocabulary in Context and Skimming and Scanning. The Skimming and Scanning Test can be found in the grade 6 materials. Some attention also might need to be paid to Word Part Clues.

Note: To find books at the *Instructional* and *Independent Reading Levels* for an individual student, go to www.harcourtachieve.com/READS.

Reading Skills and Strategies		Beginning Reader	Grade 1	Grade 2	Grade 3	Grade 4	Grade 5	Grade 6	Grade 7	Grade 8
Phonemic Awareness (Optional Test)		1-40	1-40	1-40						
Visual Discrimination		1-10	1-24	1-12						
	Single Letters		1-12	1-6						
	Letter Combinations		13-24	7-12						
Auditory Discrimination		1-10	1-24	1-20						
Initial Position	Single Consonants		1-8	1-4						
	Consonant Blends		9-12	5-8						
Final Position	Single Consonants		13-20	9-14						
	Consonant Blends		21-24	15-20						
Letter Recognition		1-10	1-26	1-26						
Sounds-Letters: Consonants		1-10	1-30	1-27	1-27	1-24	1-24			
Initial Position	Single Consonants		1-12	1-3	1-3	1-3	1-3			
	Consonant Clusters		13-18	4-9	4-6	4-6	4-6			
	Consonant Digraphs				7-9	7-9	7-9			
Final Position	Single Consonants		19-24	10-18	10-15	10-12	10-12			
	Consonant Clusters			19-27	16-21	13-15	13-15			
	Consonant Digraphs				22-27	16-18	16-18			
Rhyming			25-30							
Silent Letters						19-24	19-24			
Sounds-Letters: Vowels				1-30	1-36	1-42	1-42			
	Short Vowel a, e, i, o, u			1,3,5,6,8,10, 11,13,15, 17,19,22, 24,27,29	1,3,6,7,9, 12,13,15,18, 20,22,26, 28,32,34	1,3,5,7,9, 11,13,15,17, 19,21,25, 27,31,33	1,3,5,7,9, 11,13,15, 17,19,21, 25,27,31,33			
	Long Vowel a, e, i, o, u			2,4,7,9,12, 14,16,18, 20,21, 23,25,26, 28,30	2,4,8, 10,14,16, 19,21,24, 25,27,30, 31,33,36	2,4,6,8, 10,12,14, 16,18, 20,23,26, 29,32,35	2,4,6,8, 10,12,14, 16,18, 20,23,26, 29,32,35			
	Digraph				23,29,35	24,30,36, 38,39,40	24,30,36, 38,40,42			
	Diphthong				5,11,17	22,28,34, 37,41,42	22,28,34, 37,39,41			
Vocabulary in Context			1-15	1-22	1-22	1-22	1-24	1-24	1-24	1-24
Word Part Clues				1-21	1-24	1-24	1-18	1-18		
Affixes	Prefixes			10-15	10-15	10-15	2,4,6,8,10, 12,14,16,18	2,4,6,8,10, 12,14,16,18		
	Suffixes			1-6	5-9	7-9	1,3,5,7,9, 11,13,15,17	1,3,5,7,9, 11,13,15,17		
	Inflectional Endings			7-9	1-4	1-6				
Compound Words				16-21	16-24	16-24				

Reading Skills and Strategies		Beginning Reader	Grade 1	Grade 2	Grade 3	Grade 4	Grade 5	Grade 6	Grade 7	Grade 8
Skimming and Scanning								1-20	1-20	1-20
	Specific Details							1,3,4,5,6, 7,8,10,11, 13,15,16, 18,20	1,2,4,5,6, 7,9,10,12, 14,16,18,20	3,5,6,7,11, 12,14,15,16, 17,18,19,20
	Inference							15,16,17, 18,19	9,12,16, 19,20	2,5,8,9, 11,12,13, 14,18
	Use of Tables and Graphs							2,9,12,14	3,8,11,13, 15,17	2,4,8,13
	Overview							14,17,19	14,17,19	1,4,10
Reading Fluency (Optional Test)										
Reading Comprehension		1-5	1-44	1-49	1-45	1-48	1-48	1-48	1-48	1-45
Word Reading		5	10							
Sentence Reading		5	4	4						
Literal Comprehension			16	21	17	13	15	12	9	10
	Identify Details		1,2,3,6,7, 8,10,11,12, 13,14,16, 23,26, 28,29	1,2,3,4,7,8, 9,13,16,17, 18,19,24, 28,31,33, 41	11,14,15, 18,19,22,24, 33,34,36, 38,41,42	1,2,3,6,7, 11,12,17, 28,30, 40,46	1,2,4,7,12, 17,24,26, 30,29,40, 44	1,2,3,8, 11,19,24, 39,41, 44,45	1,7,9,18, 21,26,43	1,8,14,16, 28,29,34,36
	Recognize Sequence			15,26,27, 30	3,17,29,37	23	33,35,38	12	8,37	7,20
Inferential Comprehension			7	14	11	18	19	10	14	13
	Infer Meaning		15,20,22, 30	10,35, 40,45	5,10,30, 40,45	5,10,15,21, 32,37,43	5,10,16,21, 37,42,43,48	9,16,21, 27,43,48	11,23,30, 36,42,48	6,12,26, 32,45
	Identify Main Idea			25,34,39, 44	9,25,44	20,31,42, 47	22,32, 41	26,42	10,17,35	5,11,13, 38,40
	Identify Cause and Effect		4,5,9	12,14,29, 32,36,42	1,8,26	4,16,24,25, 29,33,45	9,11,18,19, 27,28,36,45	35,36	2,5,31, 38,40	2,18,30
Critical Comprehension			7	10	17	17	14	26	25	22
	Draw Conclusions		18,19,21, 24,25,27	5,20,21,22, 23,37,43	2,6,13,16, 20,23,39, 43	9,18,19,34, 35,36,38, 39,41,44	3,6,25,31, 34,47	4,10,15,17, 18,20,23, 25,30,33, 40,46	4,14,16,19, 20,22,27, 29,32,34, 41,46,47	3,4,9,10, 22,25,27, 31,37,44
	Summarize		17	38	12,21	13	8	5,13,14	13,28	15,19,21, 33,39
	Analyze Story Elements			6,11	4,7,27	8,22,26	13,14,20	6,7,29,31, 34,37	3,6,15,24, 33,39	
	Interpret Figurative Language				28	14,48	46		12,25	23,24,35
	Identify Author's Purpose/Audience				31,32,35		15,23	38		
	Identify Genres/Types of Passages					27		22,32,47		17
	Identify Facts and Opinions						39	28	44,45	41,42,43

Reading Skills and Strategies		Beginning Reader	Grade 1	Grade 2	Grade 3	Grade 4	Grade 5	Grade 6	Grade 7	Grade 8
Phonemic Awareness (Optional Test)		1-40	1-40	1-40						
Visual Discrimination		1-10	1-24	1-12						
	Single Letters		1-12	1-6						
	Letter Combinations		13-24	7-12						
Auditory Discrimination		1-10		1-20						
Initial Position	Single Consonants		1-8	1-4						
	Consonant Blends		9-12	5-8						
Final Position	Single Consonants		13-20	9-14						
	Consonant Blends		21-24	15-20						
Letter Recognition		1-10	1-26	1-26						
Sounds-Letters: Consonants		1-10	1-30	1-27	1-27	1-24	1-24			
Initial Position	Single Consonants		1-12	1-3	1-3	1-3	1-3			
	Consonant Clusters		13-18	4-9	4-6	4-6	4-6			
	Consonant Digraphs				7-9	7-9	7-9			
Final Position	Single Consonants		19-24	10-18	10-15	10-12	10-12			
	Consonant Clusters			19-27	16-21	13-15	13-15			
	Consonant Digraphs				22-27	16-18	16-18			
Rhyming			25-30							
Silent Letters						19-24	19-24			
Sounds-Letters: Vowels				1-30	1-36	1-42	1-42			
	Short Vowel a, e, i, o, u			1,3,5,6,8,10, 11,13,15, 17,19,22, 24,27,29	1,3,6,7,9, 12,13,15,18, 20,22,26, 28,32,34	1,3,5,7,9, 11,13,15,17, 19,21,25, 27,31,33	1,3,5,7,9, 11,13,15, 17,19,21, 25,27,31,33			
	Long Vowel a, e, i, o, u			2,4,7,9,12, 14,16,18, 20,21, 23,25,26, 28,30	2,4,8, 10,14,16, 19,21,24, 25,27,30, 31,33,36	2,4,6,8, 10,12,14, 16,18, 20,23,26, 29,32,35	2,4,6,8, 10,12,14, 16,18, 20,23,26, 29,32,35			
	Digraph				23,29,35	24,30,36, 38,39,40	24,30,36, 38,40,42			
	Diphthong				5,11,17	22,28,34, 37,41,42	22,28,34, 37,39,41			
Vocabulary in Context			1-15	1-22	1-22	1-22	1-24	1-24	1-24	1-24
Word Part Clues				1-21	1-24	1-24	1-18	1-18		
Affixes	Prefixes			10-15	10-15	10-15	2,4,6,8,10, 12,14,16,18	2,4,6,8,10, 12,14,16,18		
	Suffixes			1-6	5-9	7-9	1,3,5,7,9, 11,13,15,17	1,3,5,7,9, 11,13,15,17		
	Inflectional Endings			7-9	1-4	1-6				
Compound Words	Compound Words			16-21	16-24	16-24				

Reading Skills and Strategies	Beginning Reader	Grade 1	Grade 2	Grade 3	Grade 4	Grade 5	Grade 6	Grade 7	Grade 8
Skimming and Scanning									
Specific Details							1,3,4,5,6, 7,8,10,11, 13,15,16, 18,20	1,2,4,5,6, 7,9,10,12, 14,16,18,20	3,5,6,7,11, 12,14,15,16, 17,18,19,20
Inference							15,16,17, 18,19	9,12,16, 19,20	2,5,8,9, 11,12,13, 14,18
Use of Tables and Graphs							2,9,12,14	3,8,11,13, 15,17	2,4,8,13
Overview							14,17,19	14,17,19	1,4,10
Reading Fluency (Optional Test)									
Reading Comprehension	1–5	1–44	1–49	1–45	1–48	1–48	1–48	1–48	1–45
Word Reading	5	10							
Sentence Reading	4	4	4						
Literal Comprehension	16		21	17	13	15	12	9	10
Identify Details		1,3,4,5,6, 12,16,17, 18,19,21, 22,23	1,2,3,4,5, 8,9,12, 16,17,23, 31,32,33, 38,41	3,7,12,13, 17,18,19, 21,22,26, 27,29,37	2,3,6,8, 16,22,23, 24,31, 41,47	3,4,7,8, 9,19,23, 29,31,33, 35,40,45	2,19,20, 24,26,28, 29,30,31	7,10,14, 15,38,39 40	10,16,34, 35,38,40 41,42
Recognize Sequence			22,27, 36,37	1,11,31,32	18,27	1,12	6,40	2,31	1,3
Inferential Comprehension	7	7	14	11	18	19	10	14	13
Infer Meaning		25	15,20, 35,40,45	5,10,20,25, 30,35	5,19,20,36, 37,42,48	5,27,37, 42,43	27,32, 43,48	4,11,21, 23,29,42	39,44,45
Identify Main Idea		10,20,24	6,11,30	15	12,26, 32,35	6,22,26, 32,36,44,48	17,33,38	17,28,30	5,7,14, 21,27
Identify Cause and Effect		7,8,11	7,13,19, 21,34,42	23,38,39	1,11,13,17, 25,28,33	2,13,17,18, 20,28,30,38	11,23,45	3,8,12, 32,37	2,17,18, 30,36
Critical Comprehension	7	7	10	17	17	14	26	25	22
Draw Conclusions		2,13,14, 15,30	10,14,29, 39,44	2,4,9,14, 16,24,28, 40,41,42	4,10,21,29, 30,34,39, 44,45,46	25,34, 39,46	8,9,18, 21,22,25, 42,48	1,9,18,19, 22,24,25, 27,34,41, 45,46	4,12,19, 32,37
Summarize		9	28	34	40	15	7,34	5,33,47	23,24,31
Analyze Story Elements			18,25,26	6,8,33	7,9,15	11,24	1,12,14,39	13,16,26	8,22
Interpret Figurative Language			24	43	14	14	3,13,36	20,35,48	9,11,25,33
Identify Author's Purpose/Audience				44	38	10,47	4,10,15	6,36	13,43
Identify Genres/Types of Passages				45		16	5,16,37		6,26
Identify Facts and Opinions					43	21,41	41	43,44	15,20,28,29

Passages for the Reading Comprehension Tests: Reading Levels and Purpose Questions, Form A

Grade 1 Test		Grade 2 Test		Grade 3 Test		Grade 4 Test	
Purpose Question	**Grade**	**Purpose Question**	**Grade**	**Purpose Question**	**Grade**	**Purpose Question**	**Grade**
10 Word-Reading Items		4 Sentence Reading Items		Why did Russell feed the birds?	1	How did the kangaroo get its name?	2
4 Sentence-Reading Items		What will Father make?	Primer	Why did Max run home?	2	What was amazing about Mr. Moondrake?	3
Will Jane and Dan get the ball back?	Primer	Did the children want Rex at the party?	1	What are penguins?	2	Why does Willa think her mother should be "Father of the Year"?	3
What did Harry think he saw?	Primer	Why couldn't Ricky get to sleep?	1	Was Bingo much help?	3	Was Nasrudin telling the truth?	4
What did the children see?	1	Did Sam do a good job?	2	How do bees help flowers?	3	What did the squirrel think of the skunk?	4
What makes the ocean move?	1	How are these plants different from other plants?	2	How did these travelers get a good start in the morning?	3	Did Linda and Jane see the fog move?	4
What is Town Day?	2	Could you make this clown?	2	What is the Show-Off Show?	4	Who put the spider in Anton's bed?	5
Who does the cooking at Andrea's house?	2	What is an alphorn?	3	Why did the hiker change his mind?	4	How do you make one of these faces?	5
		Why did Isabel worry?	3	What's unusual about Venice?	5	What is it like to live under a hole in the ozone?	6
		Why do we yawn?	4				

Grade 5 Test		Grade 6 Test		Grade 7 Test		Grade 8 Test	
Purpose Question	**Grade**	**Purpose Question**	**Grade**	**Purpose Question**	**Grade**	**Purpose Question**	**Grade**
How did Joe become a hero?	3	How do chimpanzees use tools?	4	What caused these girls' near disaster?	5	Why was this train ride special?	6
How did Hippy and the monkey help each other?	4	What is cliff diving?	5	How do you make this recipe?	6	Why was Victor a lucky young man?	7/8
What kind of person was the rich man?	4	How do you make a piñata?	5	How did the writer feel about skin diving?	6	What is Douglas thinking?	7/8
What was this ocean trip like?	5	What makes geckos stick?	6	What is the purpose of this modern detective society?	7/8	Why did Nancy Elizabeth Prophet leave home?	7/8
Why should we be worried about the giant panda?	5	What problem is this teacher having?	6	What did Nicholas do?	7/8	What did this photographer's skill involve?	9/10
What is the purpose of the meeting?	5	What did the girls learn from Alana?	6	How did Tom become a teenage hero?	7/8	What are "familiar strangers"?	9/10
How are maple syrup and sugar made?	6	How do stars tell an ancient story?	7/8	How did a friend's concern change the history of the world?	9/10	What are the arguments for and against saving the courthouse?	9/10
What made this woman such a great athlete?	6	Where did we get the term *OK*?	7/8				
What steps led to the invention of the popular game *Monopoly*?	7/8	How has discus throwing changed over the years?	9/10				

Grade 1 Test		Grade 2 Test		Grade 3 Test		Grade 4 Test	
Purpose Question	Grade	Purpose Question	Grade	Purpose Question	Grade	Purpose Question	Grade
10 Word Comprehension Items		4 Sentence Comprehension Items		What did Cathy and Ringo need?	1	How does Ellen's grand-father make money?	2
4 Sentence Comprehension Items		Why didn't Pete have fun?	Pri-mer	Why did the children help the bird?	2	Did the dog find a home?	3
Which pet had the best time at the lake?	Pri-mer	What did Officer Watson do?	1	How do you make corn bread?	2	Why was this fish called Solo?	3
Why does Eva like the tree house?	Pri-mer	What does the mayor do?	1	How did the writer feel about Mr. Harby's stamps?	3	Why is eider down so expensive?	4
Why does Jenny need a better hiding place?	1	Why was Tom having trouble?	2	How are old people treated in China?	3	How did kites save this general?	4
What was Fred's trip like?	1	How did Lila feel about the rain?	2	What makes the park seem so alive?	3	Why is this a good snack?	4
What do you know about peanuts?	2	Were the wolf pups fighting or playing?	2	How did the blackbird get a drink?	4	Who was this colonial woman?	5
How did Ruth feel about flying her kite?	2	How were bricks first made and used?	3	What makes bakeries so special?	4	What does this writer want to happen?	5
		What things were different about these two vacations?	3	How did this man win a medal?	5	Why are these turtles so interesting?	6
		How do we use the cacao tree?	4				

Grade 5 Test		Grade 6 Test		Grade 7 Test		Grade 8 Test	
Purpose Question	Grade	Purpose Question	Grade	Purpose Question	Grade	Purpose Question	Grade
How did Toni pick her father's gift?	3	How does Brit feel about Amber?	4	What made Wilma a star?	5	What makes something a "Real McCoy?"	6
What is this poster about?	4	How do you make a tie-dye shirt?	5	What became of the farmer's beast?	6	What does Mille hope for?	7/8
What did they do this summer day?	4	What was the turtle's idea?	5	What was the time capsule?	6	What is the purpose of this letter?	7/8
What is the purpose of youth hostels?	5	How could your yard become a home for birds?	6	According to this poem, what was the concern of the Aztecs?	7/8	Where was the family headed?	7/8
How did Mac feel about the high dive?	5	Why would anyone want to tow an iceberg?	6	What does the girl think of the gift?	7/8	What is this film like?	9/10
How can you improve your memory?	5	What are the advantages of plywood?	6	How do you make pretzels?	7/8	What led to the creation of Frankenstein's monster?	9/10
How did Mrs. Brigley feel about owning the plates?	6	Why is the Grand Canyon special?	7/8	What is unusual about this man's hobby?	9/10	How have yo-yos changed?	9/10
Do you think you could build a gazebo?	6	What is Lizzie's problem?	7/8	What is this cleaning product like?	9/10		
Why was this American one of the greatest "all-around" athletes?	7/8	How does a ten-gear bicycle compare to a motorized bike?	9/10				

Leveling Guide: A List of Reading Level Comparisons

Rigby READS Instructional or Independent Reading Level	Rigby On Our Way to English ELL	Rigby Literacy	Fountas and Pinnell Level	Developmental Reading Assessment* (DRA) Level	Early Intervention Level (EIL, Reading Recovery)	Basal Level
Early Readiness	A	1–2	A	A/1	1	K (Readiness)
Kindergarten	B	3–4	B	2	2	K (Readiness)
1-1	C	4–7	C	3	3–4	Grade 1 (Pre-primer)
1-2	D		D	4	5–6	Grade 1 (Pre-primer)
1-3	E	7–9	E	6–8	7–8	Grade 1 (Pre-primer)
1-4	F		F	10	9–10	Grade 1 (Primer)
1-5	G	8–10	G	12	11–12	Grade 1
1-6	H		H	14	13–14	Grade 1
1-7	I	10–13	I	16	15–16	Grade 1
2-1	J		J	18	17–18	Grade 2
2-2	K	13–15	K	20	19–20	Grade 2
2-3	L		L	24		Grade 2
2-4	M	16–17	M	28		Grade 2
3-1	N	18	N	30		Grade 3
3-2	O	19	O	34		Grade 3
3-3	P	20	P	38		Grade 3
4-1	Q		Q	40		Grade 4
4-2	R		R	40		Grade 4
4-3	S		S	40		Grade 4
5-1	T		T	44		Grade 5
5-2			U, V	44		Grade 5
6-1			W			Grade 6
6-2			X			Grade 6
7			Y, Z			Grade 7
8			Y, Z			Grade 8

Levels are subjective. Adjust designated levels according to your personal evaluation.

Rigby READS Item P Values*
for Form A, Grade 5 Test

Item Number	Sounds-Letters: Consonants	Sounds-Letters: Vowels	Vocabulary in Context	Word Part Clues	Reading Comprehension Grade Level	p value
1	92	94	92	87	Grade 3	92
2	90	92	54	78		91
3	71	93	75	75		41
4	95	88	65	86		72
5	78	90	67	78		65
6	85	80	40	81	Grade 4	76
7	91	89	88	75		78
8	90	79	87	75		83
9	59	83	87	76		72
10	85	90	81	69		81
11	82	79	80	61		90
12	79	82	87	55		85
13	84	82	70	55		83
14	86	78	81	63		79
15	70	78	68	60		69
16	92	80	94	58		91
17	90	72	94	49	Grade 5	83
18	82	77	84	31		65
19	70	84	82			47
20	94	64	91			83
21	53	80	64			69
22	62	72	68			68
23	48	77	81			77
24	42	71	73			69
25		80				49
26		60				66
27		56				44
28		73				68
29		70				73
30		65				70
31		79				65
32		58				69
33		55			Grade 6	74
34		71				53
35		77				52
36		63				59
37		62				63
38		59				76
39		61				68
40		55				74
41		49				44
42		36				50
43						48
44					Grade 7-8	42
45						31
46						34
47						50
48						46

*All p values are reported without decimals. They indicate the percent of the standardization sample answering an item correctly.

Rigby READS Item P Values*
for Form B, Grade 5 Test

National Item Difficulty (p) Values by Test and Item— End of Grade 5

Item Number	Sounds-Letters: Consonants	Sounds-Letters: Vowels	Vocabulary in Context	Word Part Clues	Reading Comprehension Grade Level	p value
1	86	80	80	88	Grade 3	89
2	80	83	64	92		91
3	92	85	66	83		89
4	92	84	72	66		88
5	90	75	52	58		93
6	96	83	76	74	Grade 4	94
7	95	87	93	63		69
8	87	84	84	82		85
9	75	84	63	86		70
10	85	88	80	70		86
11	79	85	87	62		90
12	81	86	77	68		82
13	79	84	70	66		83
14	79	76	82	74		90
15	70	71	59	81		90
16	88	80	66	83		63
17	86	76	49	62	Grade 5	77
18	72	72	90	48		49
19	87	80	82			79
20	81	81	58			76
21	71	75	62			69
22	61	89	86			54
23	54	72	71			82
24	58	58	63			77
25		75				64
26		62				65
27		63				78
28		81				58
29		75				78
30		71				54
31		77				68
32		49				75
33		62			Grade 6	50
34		75				0
35		76				53
36		70				38
37		68				77
38		43				67
39		57				36
40		46				51
41		40				47
42		36				30
43						66
44					Grade 7–8	40
45						38
46						24
47						33
48						37

*All p values are reported without decimals. They indicate the percent of the standardization sample answering an item correctly.

READS Scaled Scores

The *raw score* obtained on a test is simply the number of test questions answered correctly by a student. Because the different grade levels of READS vary in length, content, and difficulty, raw scores across test levels and forms cannot be compared directly. Similarly, it is not appropriate to directly compare raw scores between the two forms—Forms A and B—of READS, even within the same grade level of the tests.

Scaled scores provide a score metric that is directly comparable across both test forms and grade levels. This makes scaled scores especially useful in gauging student growth over time—within or across school years—regardless of changes in the READS grade level or form. Raw scores are *not* appropriate for making such judgments. For example, it would not be appropriate to directly compare a raw score of 36 on the Grade 4 test to a raw score of 38 on the Grade 5 test, even if the same form of the test was used. However, it *is* appropriate to use *scaled scores* to make this comparison. Using the conversion table on the following page, a Grade 4 raw score of 36 on Form A converts to a scaled score of 131; the Grade 5 conversion of a raw score of 38 on Form A is a scaled score of 143. This indicates a growth in Reading Comprehension achievement of 12 scaled score points.

The table that follows shows conversion from a raw score to a scaled score for Reading Comprehension at each grade level for Forms A and B of READS *Evaluation* or *Diagnostic Tests*. These scores are provided only for Reading Comprehension because this is the READS component most appropriate for assessing student change or "growth" over time. READS scaled scores range from a low of 12 to a maximum score of 195. This span of points captures the entire range of achievement assessed by READS from Grades 1 through 8. Note that scaled scores are not provided for the Beginning Reader level of READS since reading comprehension is not assessed at this early level.

Scaled scores are important to users for two reasons. *First,* test levels and forms are made equivalent in the process of converting from raw score to scaled score. *Second*, scaled scores are "equal-interval" units, meaning that the amount of student growth in reading comprehension achievement indicated by a change from 40 to 45, for example, is equal to the amount of achievement change between 87 and 92.

Note that while the READS tests are grounded in the content and psychometric underpinnings of the MAT6, *Metropolitan Achievement Tests*, Sixth Edition, a test series that also provides scaled scores, the two scaled score systems differ in systematic ways. The derivation and statistical characteristics of the two sets of scaled scores are *not* comparable. Users of the MAT6 and READS tests should not attempt to mix the resulting scaled scores for the two assessments.

Rigby READS Raw-to-Scaled Score Conversion Table for Reading Comprehension

To convert an obtained raw score (number correct) to a scaled score, first find a student's raw score on either the *Evaluation Test* or the Reading Comprehension sitting of the *Diagnostic Test* in the left-most column. Then read across the table to the correct grade level and form (A or B) of READS to find the corresponding scaled score. For example, a raw score of 16 converts to a scaled score of 87 on Form A of the READS Grade 2 test or a scaled score of 120 on Form A of the Grade 7 test.

Raw Score	Grade 1 A	Grade 1 B	Grade 2 A	Grade 2 B	Grade 3 A	Grade 3 B	Grade 4 A	Grade 4 B	Grade 5 A	Grade 5 B	Grade 6 A	Grade 6 B	Grade 7 A	Grade 7 B	Grade 8 A	Grade 8 B
49			161	161												
48			153	153			174	178	184	185	185	187	190	188		
47			144	144			166	170	176	177	178	179	182	180		
46			138	138			157	161	167	168	169	171	173	172		
45			134	134	169	167	152	156	162	163	163	165	168	166	195	192
44	144	144	131	131	161	159	148	152	158	159	159	161	164	162	186	184
43	136	136	128	128	152	150	145	148	154	155	156	157	161	158	177	175
42	127	127	126	126	146	144	142	146	152	153	153	154	158	155	171	170
41	121	122	123	124	142	140	140	143	149	150	151	152	156	153	167	166
40	117	117	121	122	138	137	138	141	147	148	149	149	153	150	164	163
39	114	114	119	120	135	134	136	139	145	146	147	147	151	148	161	160
38	111	111	117	118	133	132	134	137	143	144	145	145	150	146	158	158
37	109	109	116	117	130	130	132	136	142	142	144	144	148	145	156	156
36	106	107	114	115	128	128	131	134	140	141	142	142	146	143	154	154
35	104	105	113	113	126	126	129	132	139	139	140	140	145	142	152	152
34	102	103	111	112	124	124	128	131	137	137	139	139	143	140	150	150
33	101	101	110	111	122	122	126	129	136	136	138	138	142	139	148	149
32	99	99	108	109	121	121	125	128	134	134	136	136	140	138	147	147
31	97	97	107	108	119	119	124	126	133	133	135	135	139	137	145	146
30	95	96	105	107	117	117	123	125	132	132	134	134	138	135	144	144
29	94	94	104	105	116	116	121	124	131	130	132	132	136	134	143	143
28	92	92	103	104	114	115	120	122	129	129	131	131	135	133	141	142
27	90	91	101	103	113	113	119	121	128	128	130	130	134	132	140	140
26	88	89	100	102	111	112	118	120	127	126	129	129	133	131	138	139
25	87	87	99	100	110	110	116	118	126	125	127	127	131	129	137	138
24	85	86	97	99	109	109	115	117	124	124	126	126	130	128	136	137
23	83	84	96	98	107	108	114	116	123	122	125	125	129	127	135	135
22	81	82	95	97	106	106	113	114	122	121	124	124	128	126	133	134
21	80	81	94	95	104	105	112	113	121	120	123	123	126	125	132	133
20	78	79	92	94	103	104	110	112	119	118	121	122	125	123	131	131
19	76	77	91	93	102	102	109	110	118	117	120	120	124	122	130	130
18	73	75	89	91	100	101	108	109	117	116	119	119	122	121	128	129
17	71	73	88	90	99	100	107	108	116	114	118	118	121	120	127	127
16	69	71	87	89	97	98	105	106	114	113	116	117	120	118	126	126
15	66	68	85	87	96	97	104	105	113	111	115	115	118	117	125	125
14	64	66	84	86	94	95	102	103	112	110	113	114	117	116	123	123
13	61	63	82	84	92	94	101	102	110	108	112	113	115	114	122	122
12	58	61	80	82	91	92	99	100	109	107	110	111	114	113	120	120
11	55	58	78	81	89	90	98	98	107	105	109	110	112	111	119	118
10	52	55	77	79	87	88	96	96	105	103	107	108	110	109	117	117
9	49	52	75	77	85	87	94	94	103	101	105	106	108	108	115	115
8	46	48	72	74	83	85	92	92	102	99	103	105	106	106	113	113
7	43	45	70	72	81	82	90	90	99	97	101	103	104	104	111	110
6	40	41	67	69	78	80	88	87	97	95	99	100	102	101	109	108
5	36	38	64	66	76	77	85	85	94	92	96	98	99	99	106	105
4	32	33	61	62	72	74	82	81	91	89	93	95	96	96	103	102
3	27	28	56	57	68	70	78	77	87	85	89	91	92	92	99	98
2	21	22	50	50	63	64	72	71	82	79	83	85	86	86	94	92
1	12	12	41	40	54	55	63	62	73	70	75	77	78	79	85	83

References

Informal Reading Inventories— Instructional and Independent Reading Levels

Boo, J., & Vispoel, W.P. (1998, April). *Computerized versus paper-and-pencil assessment of educational development: Score comparability and examinee preference.* Paper presented at the annual meeting of the National Council on Measurement in Education, San Diego, CA.

Bristow, P.S., Pikulski, J.J. & Pelosi, P.L. (1983). A comparison of five estimates of reading instructional level. *The Reading Teacher*, 273–279.

Bugbee, A.C. (1996). The equivalence of paper-and-pencil and computer-based testing. *Journal of Research on Computing in Education*, 28(3), 282–299.

Clay, M. M. (1993). *Reading recovery: A guidebook for teachers in training.* Portsmouth, NH: Heinemann.

Donahue, P.L., Voelkl, K.E., Campbell, J.R., & Mazzeo, J. (1999). *The NAEP 1998 Reading Report Card for the Nation and the States.* (NCES No. 1999-500), Washington, DC: U.S. Department of Education, Office of Educational Research and Improvement, National Center for Education Statistics.

Evans, L.D., Tannehill, R., & Martin, S. (1995). Children's reading skills: A comparison of traditional and computerized assessment. *Behavior Research Methods, Instruments, & Computers*, 27(2), 162–165.

Kobrin, J.L., & Young, J.W. (2003). The cognitive equivalence of reading comprehension test items via computerized and paper-and-pencil administration. *Applied Measurement in Education*, 16(2), 115–140.

Mazzeo, J., & Harvey, A.L. (1988). *The equivalence of scores from automated and conventional educational and psychological tests: A review of the literature* (College Board Rep. No. 88-8, ETS RR No. 88–21). Princeton, NJ: Educational Testing Service.

Mead, A.D., & Drasgow, F. (1993). Equivalence of computerized and paper-and-pencil cognitive ability tests: A meta-analysis. *Psychological Bulletin*, 114, 449–458.

Rasinski, T. V. (1999). Exploring a method for estimating independent, instructional, and frustration reading rates. *Reading Psychology: An International Quarterly*, 20, 61–69.

Smith, W.E. & Beck, M.D. (1980). Determining instructional reading level with 1978 Metropolitan Achievement Tests. *The Reading Teacher*, (34) 313–319.

Wise, S.L., & Plake, B.S. (1989). Research on the effects of administering tests via computers. *Educational Measurement: Issues and Practice*, 8(3), 5–10.

The Teaching and Assessment of Comprehension

National Reading Panel. (2000). *Teaching children to read*. (NIH Pub. No. 00–474). Washington, DC: National Institute of Child Health and Human Development, National Institutes of Health.

National Research Council. (1999). *Preventing Reading Difficulties*. Snow, Burns, & Griffith (Eds). Washington, DC: National Research Council.

Paris, S. G., Wasik, B. A., & Turner, J. C. (1991). The development of strategic readers. In R. Barr, M. L. Kamil, P. B. Mosenthal, & P. D. Pearson (Eds.), *Handbook of reading research*, Volume II (609–640). New York: Longman.

Pressley, M. (2000). What should comprehension instruction be the instruction of? In M.L. Kamil, P.B. Mosenthal, P.D. Pearson & R. Barr (Eds.), *Handbook of reading research*, Volume III (545–561). Mahwah, NJ: Lawrence Erlbaum Associates.

Pressley, M., Johnson, C., Symons, S., McGoldrick, J., & Kurita, J. (1989). Strategies that improve children's memory and comprehension of text. *Elementary School Journal,* 90(1), 3–32.

Pressley, M., & Woloshyn, V. (1995). *Cognitive Strategy Instruction that Really Improves Children's Academic Performance*. Cambridge, MA: Brookline Books.

Stanovich, K.E. (1986). Matthew effects in reading: Some consequences of individual differences in the acquisition of literacy. *Reading Research Quarterly*, 21, 360–407.

The Teaching and Assessment of Phonics

Armbruster, B., Lehr, F. & Osborn, J. (2001). *Put Reading First: The Research Building Blocks for Teaching Children to Read*. Washington, DC: Center for the Improvement of Early Reading Achievement and National Institute for Literacy.

National Reading Panel. (2000). *Teaching children to read*. (NIH Pub. No. 00–474). Washington, DC: National Institute of Child Health and Human Development, National Institutes of Health.

The Teaching and Assessment of Phonemic Awareness

Armbruster, B., Lehr, F. & Osborn, J. (2001). *Put Reading First: The Research Building Blocks for Teaching Children to Read*. Washington, DC: Center for the Improvement of Early Reading Achievement and National Institute for Literacy.

Juel, C. (1988). Learning to read and write: A longitudinal study of fifty-four children from first through fourth grade. *Journal of Educational Psychology*, 80, 437–447.

National Reading Panel. (2000). *Teaching children to read*. (NIH Pub. No. 00–474). Washington, DC: National Institute of Child Health and Human Development, National Institutes of Health.

Morrow, L.M. (1993). *Literacy Development in the Early Years* (2nd ed.). Boston, MA: Allyn & Bacon.

The Teaching and Assessment of Vocabulary

Beck, I.L., McKeown, M.G., & Kucan, L. (2002). *Bringing words to life*. New York: Guilford Press.

Beck, I.L. & McKeown, M.G. (1991). Conditions of vocabulary acquisition. In P.D. Pearson (Ed.), *The handbook of reading research: Vol. 2 (789–814)*. New York: Longman Press.

Blachowicz, C., & Fisher, P. (1996). *Teaching Vocabulary*. Upper Saddle River, NJ: Prentice-Hall.

Nagy, W. E. (1998). *Teaching Vocabulary to Improve Comprehension*. Newark, DE: NCTE and IRA.

National Reading Panel. (2000). *Teaching children to read*. (NIH Pub. No. 00–474). Washington, DC: National Institute of Child Health and Human Development, National Institutes of Health.

The Teaching and Assessment of Fluency

Dowhower, (1994). Repeated reading revisited: Research into practice. *Reading and Writing Quarterly*, 10, 343–358.

Fleischer, L. S., Jenkins, J., & Pany, D. (1979). Effects on poor readers' comprehension of training in rapid decoding. *Reading Research Quarterly*, 15, 30–48.

Good, R.H., Simmons, D. C. & Kame'enui, E. J. (2001). The importance and decision-making utility of a continuum of fluency-based indicators of foundational reading skills for third-grade high-stakes outcomes. *Scientific Studies of Reading*, 5(3), 257–288.

Hasbrouck, J. & Tindal, G. (1992). Curriculum-based oral reading fluency norms for students in grades 2 through 5. *Teaching Exceptional Children*, 24, 42.

Pinnell, G. S., Pikulski, J. J., Wixson, K. K., Campbell, J. R., Gough, P. B., & Beatty, A. S. (1995). *Listening to children read aloud*. Washington, DC: Office of Educational Research and Improvement, U. S. Department of Education.

Rasinski, T. V. (2000). Speed does matter in reading. *The Reading Teacher*, 54, 146–150.

Samuels, S. J. (2002). Reading fluency: Its development and assessment. In A. E. Farstrup & S. J. Samuels (Eds.), *What research has to say about reading instruction* (3rd ed., pp. 166–183). Newark, DE: International Reading Association.

Teacher's Notes

Teacher's Notes